DESIGN THINKING IN STUDENT AFFAIRS

DESIGN THINKING IN STUDENT AFFAIRS

A Primer

Julia Allworth, Lesley D'Souza, and Gavin Henning

Foreword by Janet Morrison

STERLING, VIRGINIA

Published by Stylus Publishing, LLC.
22883 Quicksilver Drive
Sterling, Virginia 20166-2019

Library of Congress Cataloging-in-Publication Data
Names: Allworth, Julia, author. | D'Souza, Lesley, author. | Henning, Gavin, author. | Morrison, Janet, Ph.D., writer of foreword.
Title: Design thinking in student affairs : a primer / Julia Allworth, Lesley D'Souza, and Gavin Henning ; foreword by Janet Morrison.
Description: First edition. | Sterling, Virginia : Stylus Publishing, LLC, 2021. | Includes bibliographical references and index. | Summary: "Design thinking is an innovative problem-solving framework. This introduction is the first book to apply its methodology to student affairs and, in doing so, points the way to its potentially wider value to higher education as a whole"-- Provided by publisher.
Identifiers: LCCN 2021034830 (print) | LCCN 2021034831 (ebook) | ISBN 9781642670325 (cloth) | ISBN 9781642670332 (paperback) | ISBN 9781642670349 (library networkable e-edition) | ISBN 9781642670356 (consumer e-edition)
Subjects: LCSH: Student affairs services. | Problem solving. | Creative thinking. | Universities and colleges--Administration.
Classification: LCC LB2342.9 .A56 2021 (print) | LCC LB2342.9 (ebook) | DDC 378.101--dc23
LC record available at https://lccn.loc.gov/2021034830
LC ebook record available at https://lccn.loc.gov/2021034831

13-digit ISBN: 978-1-64267-032-5 (cloth)
13-digit ISBN: 978-1-64267-033-2 (paperback)
13-digit ISBN: 978-1-64267-034-9 (library networkable e-edition)
13-digit ISBN: 978-1-64267-035-6 (consumer e-edition)

Printed in the United States of America

All first editions printed on acid-free paper
that meets the American National Standards Institute
Z39-48 Standard.

Bulk Purchases

Quantity discounts are available for use in workshops and for staff development.

Call 1-800-232-0223

First Edition, 2021

This book is dedicated to students. The gift of working with students is of lifelong learning, relationships, and creativity. We share back our learning to students of the past, present, and future, whose stories have the potential to shape the future of higher education as the engines of social change.

CONTENTS

FOREWORD

As a doctoral student at Bowling Green State University in the 1990s, I had the privilege of learning from Professor Carney Strange—someone I came to admire both personally and professionally. A prolific writer, renowned educator, and humanist, his work focuses on the intersection of student development, campus ecology, and multicultural pedagogy. Consistent with Lewin's 1936 equation—$B = f(p, e)$, or behavior is a function of that individual and their environment, Professor Strange studies phenomena and behaviors within the context of how learners interact with, or experience, educational environments. At the University of British Columbia in 2008, he spoke about the imperative for higher education to maintain a progressive agenda. Specifically, he said that as the ecology of a campus changes, educators and leaders must adjust to ensure that its learning environments are (re)designed not to be efficient, but rather: powerful. He underscored that all students—regardless of their identity or lived experience—must feel welcome, safe, and secure to be successful. A key to this is engaging and involving them in meaningful ways that foster a sense of deep and compelling connectedness to the institution and its membership.

Reflecting on the research I did under Carney's supervision, I see the genesis of my interest in design thinking; a problem-solving methodology grounded in genuine empathy for the students and communities we serve, a commitment to define and focus on their needs, and the cocreation of solutions for prototyping.

It's been over 20 years since I finished my PhD, but both Carney and design thinking continue to influence my leadership. Throughout my 30-year career—which has spanned seven post-secondary institutions in Canada and the United States—I have maintained a commitment to putting students and the quality of their experience at the center of my professional practice. Central to this has been an investment of time to cultivate relationships and learn from the communities I serve. This is no doubt a reflection of my training and experience in student affairs. More broadly, however, it's critical to my orientation as a transformational leader committed to encouraging, inspiring, and motivating people to drive positive personal, organizational, and social change.

Today, I proudly serve as the president and vice-chancellor of Sheridan—a learning community of approximately 40,000 full- and part-time students across three campuses in southern Ontario. I was previously the provost at Sheridan; before that, I spent 17 years at York University in Toronto, an experience that culminated in my appointment to the role of vice-provost, students. Every member of my personal or professional circle will attest to the fact that I love my work, an enthusiasm fueled by my belief in the transformative power of post-secondary education. Higher education matters because it drives personal, economic, and social outcomes for learners, families, communities, and the planet.

It is indisputable, however, that the impact of earning a college or university credential on learners is moderated—positively or negatively—by the ecology of a campus. Why, for example, are students who identify as Black or Indigenous so underrepresented in specific disciplines or programs? What determinants influence student success, broadly defined, for international students? These are, by definition, wicked problems that threaten the integrity, reputation, and sustainability of our institutions; fundamentally, they're foundational to ensuring that all learners reach their full potential. Based on my experience, the architecture of community-based problem-solving methodologies, like design thinking, offer an empathy-focused path to innovation and substantive, structural, and organizational change.

The call for higher education to adapt and respond to a changing world has never been more urgent or important. This is why this book is so salient. In the face of two global crises—the COVID-19 pandemic and a reckoning on race—our institutions must, as Veblen said in 1918, continue to facilitate "the cultivation and care of the community's highest aspirations and ideals" (p. 135). Living that potential at this moment in history rests on our commitment and capacity to engage people more fully and equitably on and beyond our campuses in assessment, planning, and change management.

The strengths of the design thinking process align well with this monumental, moral imperative. Research affirms that it can unleash creativity, enhance innovation, and promote collaboration; it can also influence leadership practice and workplace culture, both of which are keys to managing disruption and navigating change. In this context, and consistent with a quote by Coonoor Behal (2019), founder and CEO of MINDHatch, design thinking isn't about process but rather—culture:

> Design thinking isn't just a process that anyone can plug and play to get a desired output. It is much more than the process it advocates or its methods and tools. Design thinking is a way of working and behaving. It is a

mindset. It is a set of values. It requires intangibles—like humility and integrity—to do it right. (para. 8)

This speaks to why *Design Thinking in Student Affairs: A Primer* constitutes such an important and timely contribution to the literature. By focusing equally on the theory, mindset, and practice of design thinking, the book fills a gap by providing a road map for theoretically informed practice and culture change. Authored by trusted colleagues with expertise in leadership, innovation, assessment, storytelling, equity, organizational development, change management, and student success in both Canada and the United States—the book makes a compelling case for using design thinking to facilitate human-centered, cocreated, high-impact solutions within and beyond the traditional realm of student affairs.

At Sheridan, for example, we recently assembled a design team under the auspices of our "Galvanizing Education Hub" to draft short, medium, and long-term strategies to inspire and fuel our recovery from the pandemic. The design team's work was grounded in a commitment to design innovative solutions with, rather than for, the people Sheridan serves. By embracing elements of integrative thinking and human-centered design, they articulated the following challenge statement: "In the context of the current pandemic and calls for systemic change, how might we reimagine our services, outreach, programs, and teaching and learning environments to attract and support students to learn well and thrive?" After an exhausting literature review, robust engagement process, and extensive ideation, we are currently in the process of prototyping and testing solutions.

This approach can be resource intensive, but what you gain from its rigor and depth can be game-changing not only for the organization, but also for design team members. As Sheridan contemplates seismic shifts in its programs, pedagogy, and organizational structures, I see the tangible benefits of engaging our communities in the design process. To Carney's point regarding including individuals in redesigning processes, the experience served to involve people in a meaningful way that further connected them to Sheridan and its success. Simply put, they now have more stick in the game.

I want to thank the authors for their investment in the professional development of educators and leaders committed to student success. Julia, Lesley, and Gavin have earned reputations for their commitments to engagement, ethical standards, systematic inquiry to improve student and institutional performance, and building supportive, inclusive learning communities. As someone trained and grounded in the good practices for student affairs, their thought leadership aligns with my professional values and serves as much-needed inspiration. In my current role as president and vice-chancellor, their work will help me drive innovation, foster engagement, and live my reaffirmed commitments to inclusivity.

Given the unprecedented combination of new and exacerbated challenges facing our colleges and universities—decreasing government funding, student mental health and well-being, diversity and inclusion efforts, and affordability chief among them—who among us doesn't need another arrow in their quiver?

Janet Morrison
President and Vice Chancellor
Sheridan College

An idiom in higher education is that change is slow. In many ways, higher education looks very much as it did almost 2,000 years ago. A painting of a class at the University of Bologna, one of the first institutions of higher education founded in 1088, depicts a scene that mirrors one that could be found in any present-day college classroom. The instructor is on a stage lecturing to students—the infamous sage on a stage. Two students are sleeping. Two pairs of students are talking. One is looking onto the notes of the person next to them. The only things missing are electronic devices. While inventions such as online learning have changed higher education and the COVID-19 pandemic has accelerated widespread usage of remote teaching, college has remained relatively static in almost two millennia.

Major criticisms of higher education include the fact that university does not produce graduates with the skills that employers need (Andreas, 2018; NACE, 2018), that college is not worth the financial investment (Pearlstein, 2018), or that it does not meet the needs of 21st-century society (Wyman, 2018). Critics have also noted that learning in college does not seem to be a priority (Polumbo, 2018) and administrators cannot demonstrate what students have learned (Arum & Roksa, 2011; Marcus, 2018). To prepare university graduates to address global problems that do not yet exist, higher education cannot remain stagnant for another 2,000 years. Rather, higher education must innovate. Colleges and universities must not only innovate their operations but also their organizational structures. Design thinking constitutes one approach to innovation which also cultivates skills and competencies in students to be critical thinkers.

This is the context that provides the foundation for our own experiences with design thinking. Each of our journeys is different and thus the perspectives we have on design thinking vary.

Julia Allworth

To me, design thinking happens in practice. I am a practitioner of design thinking, learning as I go. My undergraduate work at Western University in Ontario, Canada focused on psychology. I have always been fascinated by people, organizations, and how change happens. I am also a single mom of twins who due to their premature birth have many learning differences, so I am passionate about universal design and how design thinking can be used to create solutions that benefit people whose needs are considered different. After many years of working in various leadership roles in both private and public sector education starting with K–12 and later in higher education, I returned to school and completed an MBA from the University of Fredericton, seeking to understand how innovation and systems change could be operationalized in higher education.

While leading the Employer Recruitment and Engagement team at the University of Toronto's Career Centre, I could often see that students did not feel fully prepared for their life beyond university. I thought a lot about how students and the world were rapidly changing, and how institutions of higher education needed to change with them. I took courses in strategy and innovation in business school around this time and thought deeply about how institutions of higher education are so different from the corporate world. Decisions are made differently and people work together differently. Still, I continued to think that change was needed and possible, and I was driven to discover how real and meaningful change could happen in a large, decentralized institution like the University of Toronto.

In 2016 I was given the opportunity to launch a new initiative: The Innovation Hub at the University of Toronto. Inspired by the book, *Leading Innovation and Change: A Guide for Chief Student Affairs Officers on Shaping the Future* (Smith et al. 2015) and a related conference at NASPA around that time, Heather Kelly and David Newman, both senior directors of the Division of Student Life at the University of Toronto, imagined the Innovation Hub as a space where human-centered design thinking could be used to explore two key questions: *Who are our students? How is the world changing for them?* Entrusted to design and lead the Innovation Hub, I gathered input from students, staff, and faculty about their priorities and designed a student-led work-integrated learning program where interdisciplinary teams of students from all degree programs and study levels are trained in design thinking. These teams of students work directly with campus partners who have a project or initiative where they want to understand their stakeholders more deeply.

Over the past 5 years, the Innovation Hub has become a well-known and trusted initiative on our campus. I believe that this trust comes from our student-centric values as well as the institutional knowledge that we have acquired through hundreds of in-depth conversations with students and others about their experiences (The Innovation Hub, 2019). Additionally, we have been fortunate to welcome hundreds of students as team members i over the years, and many are skilled qualitative researchers who have helped us to refine our unique approach to design thinking, which places strong emphasis on the initial insights phase of the process and collecting data with integrity. The Innovation Hub offers valuable learning opportunities for students where they have a chance to address real-world problems that actually impact them using design thinking. Many of the students I have worked with are now successfully working in innovation and design-thinking or user-experience roles across North America.

Throughout the book, I draw on examples from work that my students have done at the University of Toronto Innovation Hub. I hope that these examples will bring to life the concepts presented throughout the book as illustrations and examples of one application of design thinking in a higher education context. I wish to acknowledge, however, that there are many incredible design thinkers working in education spaces and examples of design thinking done well in higher education are plentiful.

My hope is that this book offers inspiration to student affairs practitioners and leadership in all areas that innovation is possible in higher education. My experience is that launching new methods for innovation such as design thinking requires strong leadership and championing, which I have been fortunate enough to receive at the University of Toronto. In the following pages, my coauthors and I will share our combined knowledge on this topic and offer what we hope is a detailed examination of how design thinking can create change by generating deep empathy for students and their needs and translating the information gathered into insights that lead to new possibilities in the future.

As a design thinking practitioner, and as someone who has trained countless students and professionals in the process, I feel it is also important to note this book's bias toward a focus on empathy in design thinking. There are so many important aspects of design—why focus so much on empathy above other important concepts in design thinking such as prototyping and testing? There is no more important time for change in higher education than in this current moment. With systems and structures in our institutions being largely top-down, using empathy in design thinking is disruptive and can flip things on their head. The focus that design places on bringing the people into the process and designing with them, rather than for them, through a process that generates a deeper understanding of human needs is a much-needed change in our context.

Lesley D'Souza

I am a Canadian student affairs professional, having worked in the field for 16 years at six different institutions in Canada and the United States. I received my master's degree in college student personnel from Bowling Green State University and I am the mother of two young boys. I came to student affairs from an undergraduate degree in biology where I explored the living world through scientific method and learned to seek data to substantiate our hypotheses. As I began my career as a new student affairs professional, I constantly struggled with how we could truly understand the impact of our work—what perfect experiments could we design that could possibly get at the complex nature of personal growth and learning? In 2016 assessment became my full-time job as I joined the ranks of assessment professionals. This was a joyful reunion, and I was finally able to apply myself to exploring my work using my background in science and newly acquired skills in development of learning outcomes and qualitative assessment. I would still be doing the work the same way was it not for deep conversations and transformational learning that happened with Indigenous colleagues. My job title was Manager of Student Affairs Storytelling, and the naming of this role propelled me into a journey learning about storytelling and its Indigenous roots. I began to deconstruct all the things that I thought I knew about knowledge and took active steps to learn about Indigenous pedagogy. Once I did so, I started to ask questions about the colonial nature of the very assessment work I felt so passionate about. Why was I creating assessments that failed to make space for students to be part of establishing value and standards for their own knowledge? Why were they so often absent from the analysis and interpretation of data that they had contributed to? Were we serving students—equity-seeking students in particular—well if that data was being used to support decisions that were imposed upon them, rather than built with them? So, when a colleague sent me an article with the Stanford d.school design thinking process, I was primed to see the parallels to our assessment cycle, but the naming of empathy as a vital part of the process was an epiphany. I had been connecting storytelling to empathy without language to bring empathy into the foundational assessment processes that we were building, and it was a short leap to connect the two. This book brings together the knowledge that I have been so lucky to have amassed from students, friends, and colleagues over the last 16 years. It does not belong to only me, though it is my privilege to have undertaken the labor to share what I have learned. Design thinking on its own is not a magic solution to our most tangly problems. Using design thinking models as a basis for building interventions in higher education presents opportunities to not only build innovative and disruptive solutions, but also change the way we think. I hope the next pages bring new knowledge to add to your own and that this becomes part of your own journey to be positive changemakers in the world.

Gavin Henning

I never intended on going into student affairs as a career. Thirty years after finishing a bachelor's degree in psychology and sociology, here I am. Still. While I am a full-time faculty member, and have been for 9 years, I see myself as a scholar-practitioner. Most of my 20 years as a higher education administrator was spent doing assessment work where I was tasked with applying and helping others apply data for decision-making and quality improvement. In my scholarship, I write for practitioners, focusing on practical applications of assessment.

A few years ago, I stumbled upon a TED Talk by Tim Brown (2009-b), executive chair of IDEO, the storied design firm, and was fascinated by the concept of design. As a result, I read his book *Change by Design* (2009-a).

I didn't fully realize the application of design and particularly design thinking to higher education until I met Lesley. She described how design thinking could be applied to assessment in higher education. She explained how the processes were similar and how design thinking could improve how practitioners had been implementing assessment. After dipping my toes in the literature, I realized pretty quickly the applicability of design thinking to many aspects of student affairs work beyond assessment, including programming and problem-solving. Collaborating with and learning from Julia and Lesley has confirmed for me the untapped potential for design thinking in student affairs and higher education.

The three of us approached this book from both practical and academic perspectives. Design thinking is a practice. However, given the newness of the topic to higher education and student affairs, we wanted to make a strong academic case for its usage. Readers may perceive this tension at various points throughout the book.

We would like to note some issues with design thinking language; while some terminology such as "user" and "end-user" may not align with inclusion and equity, we have decided to employ this terminology used in design thinking.

Design thinking is a process primarily used for problem-solving that is rooted in creative fields such as art and design. Typically a five-step process, design thinking includes the following steps: (a) empathize with users to learn about their experiences in relation to the problem or issue, (b) define the problem or issue, (c) ideate potential solutions, (d) prototype and test solutions, and (e) invest in a solution to implement. While the approach has been adapted to business, despite its limitations design thinking applies to higher education and student affairs specifically as it aligns well with the latter's values and is easily adapted for the development of new programs, services, and initiatives.

Because of its focus on empathy, which is the need to thoroughly understand users' experiences, design thinking is user-centered similar to how student affairs is student-centered. Because the focus of design thinking is to design *with* users, not *for* users, it aligns well with student affairs practice. In addition, the focus on empathy makes design thinking a more equitable approach to problem-solving than other methods because all users' experiences—not just typical users' experiences—need to be understood. Authentic voices of all must be heard. As a result, centering empathy in problem-solving processes can be a tool to disrupt higher education systems and practices. The solution ideation or development process is data-driven and considers both qualitative and quantitative data as both are needed to provide the most complete picture of the issue and possible solutions. Neither quantitative nor qualitative data alone can do this. Design thinking includes a step for prototyping and testing of prototypes. The prototyping step helps ensure that an innovation is not scaled up until it has been tested and revised based on feedback mirroring processes in higher education assessment and improvement science. While design thinking takes more time to implement than other problem-solving strategies, resources are better utilized because of the extensive data collection, analysis, and testing that takes place, leading to a high-quality product or service that truly addresses needs of users.

In addition to being an innovative problem-solving framework, design thinking is a unique approach to student engagement. Students are cocreators during the design process. Involving students in the design thinking process provides them agency through the process and teaches them design thinking through their own participation. Thus, design thinking can address an issue through the development of a product, program, or service and is a way to engage students.

Design thinking can also be applied to assessment processes building on a traditional assessment framework that centers on four key steps: (a) develop outcomes, (b) deliver strategies to achieve outcomes, (c) measure data to determine outcome effectiveness, and (d) implement change as a result of the data. Design thinking assessment offers a more inclusive and equitable approach to assessment supporting recent trends regarding equity-minded assessment.

Design thinking has numerous benefits to afford students affairs. The following pages outline the basic tenets of design thinking along with applications to student affairs. Chapter 1 outlines a case for design thinking in student affairs. Chapter 2 discusses a brief history of design thinking, noting its germination and evolution to current practice. Chapter 3 provides a detailed description of each step of the design thinking model with pertinent examples to make the steps clearer. Chapter 4 explains the intersection of equity and design thinking while chapter 5 explores the use of design thinking for organizational change. Chapter 6 presents a new model for design thinking assessment. Chapter 7 addresses the challenges and limitations of the process. Chapter 8 concludes the book by discussing the alignment of design thinking and student affairs and outlining next steps. Design thinking is an innovative process that can change the way higher education and student affairs operate while realizing the potential it offers.

ACKNOWLEDGMENTS

Design thinking is hailed as an inclusive approach to solving complex problems. One reason inclusion is valued in the design thinking process is because solutions require input from multiple perspectives and utilization of varied talents. Producing this book was no different.

We wanted to acknowledge the individuals who played a part in the publication of this book. Some friends and colleagues served as sounding boards for ideas, shared expertise, or directed us to critical resources. Others played a more substantial role in volunteering to review the book and provide candid and critical feedback. Their thoughtful insights were invaluable as we attempted to make this book as accessible and useful as possible. Thank you to Jeff Burrow, Aayan Hagar, Terri Greene Henning, Heather Kelly, Nogah Kornberg, Anne Lundquist, David Newman, Adam Peck, Sylvia Spears, Nico Waltenbury, and Heather Watts for making this publication better through your expert feedback.

As settlers, we acknowledge our relationship to the land we are privileged to live upon and the Indigenous peoples who have shaped what we understand about collective knowledge and storytelling.

We would also like to thank John von Knorring at Stylus Publishing for being open to this novel idea for a book and supporting us through the process.

THE CASE FOR DESIGN THINKING IN HIGHER EDUCATION AND STUDENT AFFAIRS

P oor graduation rates are a topic on most college campuses. Senior administrators understand the importance of retention and graduation rates because graduation rates mean more money through revenue generation and possibly increased state funding, which can fund priorities across the institution including faculty research, student scholarships, and staffing for student support services. While campus resources are important, there are broader implications of college degree attainment for students. Individuals with a college degree have higher earnings than those who do not (National Center for Education Statistics, 2020). They also have better health, housing, and employment benefits (Ma et al., 2016). In addition to individual benefits, there are societal benefits for increased college graduation rates. Higher earnings lead to higher taxes being paid to support public programs (Ma et al., 2016). Individuals with college degrees are less likely to be on public assistance and are healthier, which lowers health-care costs (Ma et al., 2016). Since the establishment of the earliest colleges in the United States, women, Black, Indigenous, and People of Color (BIPOC) have been excluded from and minoritized within higher education. Design thinking can be an inclusive process that addresses the complex problems of equity in colleges and universities. While many institutional leaders realize the many benefits for their institutions, their students, and society of improving their graduation rates, they are stuck as to how to go about addressing this problem. Design thinking is a possible approach.

Design thinking is a human-centered approach to innovation that emphasizes building empathy for user needs. Design thinking is a shift away from traditional top-down approaches to product and service design in favor of a more user-centered approach. This chapter introduces design thinking as a creative problem-solving process that emphasizes a focus on building a deeper understanding, or empathy, for the people who will benefit from the design. The argument for the application of design thinking in a student affairs context is one that sets the stage for the deeper examination of design thinking and applications of the process in student affairs throughout the book.

Design thinking has been a staple in the creative world of design, but virtually unknown in higher education and student affairs. As a problem-solving approach, it has the potential to transform higher education by increasing effectiveness through equitable solutions. Design thinking aligns well with student affairs as there are numerous shared values. Design thinking is person-centered just as student affairs is student-centered. Design thinking is a people-based, not technology-based, problem-solving approach that begins with empathizing to gain a deep understanding of the needs of users. The process is inclusive and collaborative, like action research where participants are involved in developing a solution to a problem or issue that directly affects them. As such, there is a focus on equity because the goal is to find solutions for all users—solutions for those on the outer tips of the bell curve, not just for the majority in the center of the curve. Because the approach is inclusive, collaborative, and people-centered, the process is as important as the solution.

Design thinking's focus on process mirrors student affairs work. Student affairs professionals either directly or indirectly strive to foster student learning and development, which is a process. These staff are not building widgets. The product for student affairs is not students, but their learning and development.

Design thinking also considers culture and context. Neither individuals nor problems exist in vacuums. Elements of culture, such as values, beliefs, assumptions, symbols, and language all affect the way a problem manifests as well as the way a problem or issue may be addressed. These cultural elements need to be made explicit in the emphasizing phase and attended to in the ideation, prototyping, and testing phases of design thinking. A cultural approach to problem-solving is applicable to student affairs because offices, departments, and programs exist in organizations that have multiple layers of culture.

Design thinking is also a process that reduces risk. The purpose of prototyping is to test out solutions before scaling them up for the larger population. The design thinking approach is beneficial in a higher education setting where resources are scarce. In an environment with limited resources, it is better to test out a minimal viable product than go to scale and then realize that there is a problem in the product, program, or service that could have easily been addressed during a prototype phase. Willingness to fail and abandon a tested program or service in favor of something that will be more desirable, feasible, and viable is an important mindset in design thinking. Given the underlying values of design thinking and the characteristics of the process, it fits well with student affairs and higher education.

Finally, design thinking offers rich learning and collaboration opportunities for students. Across institutions there are thousands of talented students seeking meaningful applied learning opportunities. Learning the design thinking process and having the opportunity to work with other students, staff, and faculty on a collaborative and interdisciplinary team is a powerful experience. The opportunities to bring diverse stakeholders into a design process align with the collaborative and consultative cultures at many institutions of higher education. These features of the process are also in alignment with the commitment and value that most institutions place on developing rich learning experiences for students.

At the University of Toronto Innovation Hub, teams of interdisciplinary students work together on projects that impact them in a consulting model, partnering with divisions and departments on campus who want to better understand stakeholder needs and innovate. This ranges from space redesign projects to new programs and services or investments in other innovations. Each student brings their unique experiences and theoretical lens from their area of study to the process, which helps them see their academic knowledge through a new lens. They also have the opportunity to see the importance of context when learning about the complexity of the issues through the eyes of stakeholders who have divergent opinions and viewpoints. Bringing students into a design team offers them practical skills which help them better understand who they are, how they work in a team context, and why complex problems are so challenging to solve.

What Is Design Thinking?

Design thinking is a creative, inclusive problem-solving process that emphasizes a focus on the people who are the beneficiaries of the design. With an emphasis on building empathy for end users as part of the information gathering process, design thinking prioritizes the discovery and deeper understanding of human needs to ensure that innovative solutions are desirable to users. While traditional problem-solving approaches tend to focus on quickly identifying the problem to be solved and moving straight to a solution, the design thinking process encourages building empathy and taking more time to define the problem as viewed from the end user perspective before building solutions. Design thinkers at global design firm and innovation company IDEO (2019) suggest that true innovation happens at the intersection of desirability, feasibility, and viability. A solution to any problem is only innovative when it is:

- desirable, or something the beneficiary of the design really wants and that will meet their needs;
- feasible, or something that can really be done given available resources, systems, and other enabling factors; and
- viable, so something that will advance the goals of the organization and where gains from implementing the solution will bring enough value to justify investments of time and resources (Van Tyne, 2016).

The design process, when regarded through the lens of desirability, feasibility, and viability, provides a recipe for steps to be taken to better define complex problems and generate innovative solutions.

Design thinking consists of five steps: empathize, define, ideate, prototype, and test. First, empathize with users to understand the problem or issue; using what was learned in the empathize phase, define the issue or problem to be addressed through the design thinking process; ideate possible solutions to the problem or issue; prototype solutions which could be a product, program, or service; and test the prototypes making improvements (see Figure 1.1).

Figure 1.1. Design thinking process.

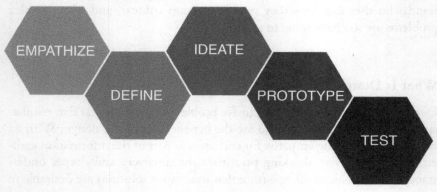

While the model is often depicted as a linear process, frequently previous steps are revisited. After testing a prototype and learning that it does not address the problem, designers may revisit the ideate step to explore additional potential solutions. A prototype may be tested multiple times after improvements are engineered after each testing phase. Sometimes, designers must go back to the empathize step to further explore the issue to more precisely define the problem. Design thinking is a somewhat cyclical process.

Practitioners may find the steps in design thinking easily understood and intuitive and some may argue that design thinking is common sense. Many practitioners may think they are using design thinking even if they are not following the steps outlined in chapter 3. While easy to understand as a process, design thinking proves more difficult to implement.

There are five key characteristics of design thinking: its use to address wicked problems, use of empathy, a collaborative approach of designing with people rather than for people, design thinking as both a method and mindset, and the emphasis on failure as learning.

Wicked Problems and Design Thinking

It is impossible to discuss design thinking without introducing the concept of a wicked problem. The term has been attributed to planner Horst Rittel (1973) to describe problems that are extremely complex in nature and seem near impossible to solve. Higher education is full of wicked problems. These wicked problems are highly ambiguous, and there are just as many unknown factors as those that are known. There are no clear yes or no solutions to wicked problems. In fact, some of the better solutions often reveal more underlying problems and design challenges.

To add to the complexity of wicked problems, a solution that works today may prove obsolete in the future, and one solution may work only in a certain context but not in others. The information about the problem can be contradictory and confusing, and there are often many decision makers and stakeholders whose values and priorities conflict with one another (Transition Design Seminar, 2020). Wicked problems are nonlinear and complex. Wicked problems require deep inquiry and layers of empathy building prior to solution generation. It is important that the problem is as well-defined as possible before generating solutions to wicked problems. Design thinking helps teams to better define problems.

When thinking about the current state of student affairs in higher education, many examples come to mind. Take, for example, the complexity of student mental health. Campuses and university administrators across the world are struggling to understand and address the issue of mental health. The *Higher Ed Today* survey of presidents on college student mental health and well-being indicated that over the last 10 years student mental health concerns have escalated, and death by suicide is the number two cause of death for college students (Chessman & Taylor, 2019). This perception is supported by data from the National College Health Association. In spring 2016, 14% of respondents reported being diagnosed for depression (American College Health Association [ACHA], 2016) compared to 22% in spring of 2020 (ACHA, 2020). Student mental health is a complex topic, and there are many complicated factors that come into play. College and university administrators cannot simply think about mental health as a medical issue; they must look at the landscape for today's students: interpersonal and family relationships, community dynamics, social support, and school conditions (Office of Disease Prevention and Health Promotion [ODPHP], 2020).

There is a long list of factors that impact student mental health including the stakeholders who play different roles in the system that supports students during their time in higher education. These factors combine to suggest that mental health is a wicked problem with no simple solution. Addressing this issue requires a quest for deeper understanding of the causal issues at play and building empathy for the various stakeholders to develop an appreciation for the complexity of the issue. Design thinking addresses these types of wicked problems.

Empathy and Design Thinking

Central to design thinking is a fundamental shift in the approach to innovation, problem-solving, and creating that can be summarized in a simple phrase: Design thinking is designing *with* rather than *for* people (IDEO U, 2017), highlighting the importance of empathy in the process in a way that makes empathy an action word. As noted earlier, in design thinking, the members of the population impacted by the design process are invited to become active participants in the process. The use of empathy acknowledges that people hold the solutions to their problems and that through engagement with people there can be collective discovery of new solutions that better meet needs. Ultimately, empathy is about understanding the logics, experiences, worldviews, identity, needs, and desires of people. Empathy also requires deep listening and observation as tools to learn about the experiences of others.

A particularly heartwarming example of empathy comes from a project shared with one of the authors with Nogah Kornberg, assistant director of I-Think, a nonprofit initiative making real-world problem-solving core to every classroom. Students are taught design thinking and integrative thinking in K–12 classrooms and given real problems from real organizations where they apply their learning and recommend innovations to the organization. In this example, students at John Polanyi Collegiate Institute in Rahim Essabhai's class were working on a problem with the community garden at the school, run by a local nonprofit. The issue was that at night people from the community were coming and picking vegetables but were doing so improperly and causing damage to the vegetable plants. Students needed to build empathy for the people who were damaging these plants in order to find an appropriate solution.

Students chose to attend a Toronto Community Housing meeting to understand the issues that residents of the community faced. During the meeting that the students attended, there was a focus on the experience of seniors being isolated, especially in the winter. Senior members of the community shared their experiences at the meeting. The issue of isolation with seniors was particularly concerning, especially in a community where the residents had a great deal of respect for their elders.

After attending the Toronto Community Housing meeting, the students decided that the learning they had experienced about seniors would be important as they developed their solution. The problem the students initially set out to solve was the issue of the vegetable picking at night causing damage to the plants, yet the students felt deep empathy for the seniors in the community. Compelled to address the issue of isolation that these seniors faced, the students used this information to form their solution. They decided that if the garden was rebranded as a garden for seniors, where they could come and socialize while caring for the plans, it would generate enough respect that the community members would learn how to properly interact with the plants to maintain the health of the garden. By engaging in empathy building as a part of their design thinking experience, students were able to create recommendations for the community garden that reflected the culture of the community.

Each individual brings their own mental models, a lens through which they view the world, into the design thinking process. Daniel Kahneman's work provides useful research that helps give additional insight into how mental models work. In his book *Thinking Fast and Slow*, Kahneman (2011) suggested that there are two modes of thinking that the brain is capable of. Over decades of research, Kahneman has shown that there is a dichotomy between System 1 thinking, which is fast, emotional, and based on instinct and System 2 thinking, a more deliberate and slower, logical thought process.

In day-to-day life, including life within the workplace, System 1 thinking is commonplace: thinking that is automatic and repetitive, often unconscious. Driving on a highway, addressing emails with the same type of greeting, making quick decisions based on reasoning, and making small talk all rely on some form of automatic thinking that comes naturally and requires minimal mental exertion. System 1 thinking is beneficial as it helps with day-to-day functioning by automatizing what can be automatic and helping our brain make pathways to understanding the world. To do problem definition well, one must enter into System 2 thinking, which is a slower, more methodical, and effortful process, such as when we solve complex mathematical equations, dig into our memory to recognize a familiar yet unknown sound or scent, or try to listen to what someone is saying in a loud environment (Kahneman, 2011).

When carrying out design thinking processes, an equity-centered approach allows design teams to practice examining their own implicit and explicit biases and bring an awareness of these to the foreground. For this reason, the second feature of design thinking is that it encourages intentionality in selecting an appropriate team and requires the right people to be brought into the process.

Designing *With* Rather than *for* People

One of the fundamental concepts in design thinking is that a strong design process seeks to bring the end user into the process in an authentic way. The phrase designing with rather than designing for is widely recognized in the design community as an ideal to strive for. In design thinking, every effort is made to bring the populations who are impacted by and who would benefit from the end design into the design process. Engagement with users is built into the process, but consideration is also given to how to include these users as active and valued members of the design team, often leading the design team, to ensure that the process is highly inclusive and that their participation is meaningful.

In a higher education context, there is a great deal of discourse about students: what they want, what they need, what might be best for them. Often this discourse takes place among faculty and staff administrators and can fail to engage the students themselves. In design thinking, every effort is made to bring students into the process in meaningful ways rather than making assumptions based on past experiences with students and/or anecdotal information. Engaging students is important for a few reasons. The primary reason is that students have the most valuable experiences that can contribute to insights about what they need: their own lived experience. The second reason is much more practical: "People will support what they create" (IDEO U, 2017, para. 11). Design thinking encourages leaders to think about building teams of designers that are at least partially composed of the people who will benefit from the end design.

Design Thinking—Both a Method and a Mindset

Design thinking offers a method for innovation built on principles of empathy building. As a method, it provides a set of iterative steps that are intended to help the designer: (a) to better understand the needs of the people who will benefit from the design, (b) to use that information to better define the problem being solved, (c) to take that information and use it to inspire new idea generation, and (d) to test those ideas in the form of prototypes (Battarbee et al., 2015). There are several models for design thinking described in the following pages that outline a particular method for doing design thinking work, each framed in a slightly different way.

Design thinking has also come to be appreciated not only as a method but also a mindset. It is a recipe for creativity whereby the designer at first is like someone cooking a recipe for the first time, following every instruction carefully in sequence. Over time, the idea is that the same person will perfect the recipe to their own liking, becoming like a chef who can make the dish without a recipe and have it turn out even better (Carter, 2016). At first in design thinking, the methodology is important as the designer employs the tools that the method offers in sequence to go through the process. Over time, with more design projects completed, designers start to use the process out of sequence, or bring elements of the process into day-to-day life. Using design thinking more comfortably and more naturally is what is meant by having a design thinking mindset. With empathy building, learning from frequent failure, and iteration based on these learnings as core concepts, design thinking mindsets can support designers in their day-to-day roles as well as when undertaking a large-scale design process. Design thinking as a mindset can be achieved only through practice.

Failure as Learning

A final defining feature of design thinking is its emphasis on failure as learning. IDEO U (2017) encourages designers to reframe failure as learning by thinking about solution generation as an experiment or prototype rather than as a one-time practice. Embedded in the design thinking process is an expectation that there are many possible solutions to each problem, and the best way to find the appropriate solution is by creating models or prototypes of an idea to test with the people who will be using the solution. Their criticism of the prototype can be regarded as valuable feedback and additional empathy building information that can be creative fuel for refined prototypes. A defining feature of the design thinking process is that solutions are never final, and there is always room to make changes (IDEO U, 2017).

Why Design Thinking in Student Affairs

Design thinking can be a powerful tool for use in student affairs and other areas of higher education. Design thinking is particularly helpful to student affairs for four main reasons: (a) it is a method for creative problem-solving to address complex problems in the field, (b) the approach aligns with cultural values of student affairs practice, (c) it is a strategy to foster equity and inclusion, and (d) it can be applied to assessment practice as a strategy for accountability and improvement in the field.

The higher education landscape is constantly changing due to student needs, new governmental policies, and other internal and external factors. Student retention and graduation rates is a top issue for colleges as is the need for colleges to further critical thinking skills (Haber, 2020). The financial impact of the 2008 recession caused institutions to scale back programs and services, reallocate resources, and for some, close their doors. The outbreak of the COVID-19 pandemic in spring 2020 shifted on-campus teaching and involvement to remote learning and engagement almost overnight and changed higher education. The pandemic also negatively affected college enrollments for fall 2020 (Douglas-Gabriel, 2020). Given the decreased enrollments resulting from the recession and the COVID-19 pandemic, retention and graduation rates have become even more important than ever before. Student retention and graduation rates, the COVID-19 pandemic, and financial constraints could be considered wicked problems because they are complex with multiple origins and do not have an easily identifiable solution. Further complicating this is the fact that these three issues are interconnected with each affecting the other two. Each of these problems requires a creative, innovative, and broad constituency-supported approach to resolution. Design thinking is a process tailored to address these kinds of complex problems.

Design thinking is culturally aligned with student affairs values. Students are the center of student affairs work. Many professionals enter the field because they had a mentor who was empathetic and supportive when they were students and these professionals want to serve in the same role for other students. Empathy is at the heart of student affairs work as supporting students proves difficult if one cannot understand what students experience and feel, or anticipate issues they will encounter. Equity and inclusion form the foundation of student affairs work as professionals in the field work diligently to ensure all students, regardless of their identity, are afforded the same opportunities for development and growth. Policy and program development are more effective and equitable if diverse student voices are included, which is also a tenet of design thinking. Collaboration is a key tool in student affairs work, helping to ensure multiple perspectives. Wicked problems cannot be solved by one person alone; a team, with varied expertise and diverse viewpoints working together, is needed. Design thinking is an inclusive process built on empathy with end user voices included to ensure the development of the best intervention, program, or service to address the issue at hand. But it is also a vehicle for equity because it can address issues of power and oppression. Design thinking is more equitable in both process and product. Similar to most approaches to address equity, design thinking is a time-intensive process. But dismantling systems of power and oppression are worthy of the requisite time and energy. The relational, student centered, inclusive principles of design thinking make it a problem-solving approach well-aligned with student affairs work.

In addition to being used for problem-solving, design thinking supplements traditional assessment processes. Assessment has become a key function in student affairs, used as a tool to demonstrate value, articulate the connection of student affairs work to the educational mission of the institution, identify opportunities for improvement, and share the "story" of student affairs to multiple constituencies. Integration of design thinking into the traditional assessment process expands that process by incorporating key steps such as empathy, prototyping, and testing. Design thinking assessment is more aligned with student affairs work than traditional assessment rooted in academic processes, because empathy as well as program/service development are key components of the adapted assessment cycle.

Creators Support What They Create

The design thinking process focuses on empathy building for users, which allows a deeper insight to be gleaned about what this population really needs. For this reason, it is different from other traditional assessment efforts. For example, surveys generally focus on asking pointed questions where respondents are asked to provide a ranking of a predetermined criteria or phrase, or ask for short answers to questions that can be focused on solutions. Where open-ended questions exist, rarely do they yield deep information as to why respondents said what they did, and they lack the opportunity to ask deeper probing questions to get to core human needs. Often, when this kind of information is needed, institutions choose to run focus groups. In a focus group, the conversation may tend to be top-down and driven based on the specific questions that the group seeks to answer. Often the questions may be framed as asking participants what they want or what they think is needed. While there is certainly a place for these methods and they are excellent ways to consult with stakeholders, design thinking takes a different approach.

Design thinking seeks to engage teams in a creative process of curiosity, an active approach to better understanding a person or population of persons (IDEO U, 2017). Design thinking takes an open-ended, constructivist approach to conversations with stakeholders in an attempt to uncover information the team did not know that it did not know. The inquiry is participant-driven and open-ended. In fact, the problem definition phase in design thinking happens after the data is collected.

When the design team includes individuals who self-identify as being members of the population impacted by the design, they essentially are designing for themselves. This is a powerful concept in design. The idea is that when members of the population are engaged in a process of solving their own problems, the likelihood that the solution will be successful, or the extent to which it will be taken up by the wider population, is higher.

Sometimes, traditional program and service design looks like professionals taking a parental approach that comes with the belief of knowing what someone needs or what is best for that person or group of people. Design thinking opens up the possibility that by working together with the persons impacted by a problem or a situation, there can be a collective discovery of the solution through immersive experiences and information gathering followed by group analysis to define a problem and look for new and emergent ways to solve the problem, or at least approach it differently. This process can feel uncomfortable and requires a mindset shift. Egos and individual contributions must be set aside in this process, as it quickly becomes evident that the divergent and contradictory perspectives and opinions of various individuals involved can become assets rather than barriers to innovation.

The idea that creators support what they create differentiates design thinking from other methods. The design team is composed of those impacted directly by the problems that the process seeks to solve. The investment of time and energy into the process create a level of commitment to supporting the outcome. Additionally, understanding why something happens the way it does or why something is done in a certain way is powerful context. Participation in a design process creates contextual understanding and commitment to supporting whatever the process produces and therefore the creators ultimately support their own creation.

Design thinking, while developed in the business world, applies to the student affairs world. The wicked problems in the field can only be solved through an innovative, equitable, user-centered approach such as design thinking. The following chapters will explicate the application of design thinking to student affairs by providing a primer on the topic for the field.

2

DESIGN THINKING

A Brief History

T he term *design thinking* often surfaces thoughts about the corporate world and how Fortune 500 companies have brought innovation into their plans to increase profits and shareholder value. In relation to student affairs and higher education, the goals are quite different than corporate goals, and so the term itself can seem corporate or distasteful to those who are unfamiliar with its origins and intended purpose. It is important to note that design thinking is not without criticism and a full discussion of criticism and challenges with design thinking is discussed later in the book.

Design thinking has a history that has emerged from various fields of study and a variety of applications. There is no one person or industry completely credited with initiating design thinking. Ironically, the ideas, processes, and associated mindsets around design thinking have undergone many iterations and applications over the decades. The history of design thinking seems like a series of prototype theories, models, and ideas that have been tested, refined, and retested. The history of design thinking is true to a concept that is foundational in its intent: failing toward success (Crabtree, 2017). That learning happens through failure is an important idea throughout design thinking's history.

Where Did Design Thinking Come From?

References to the term *design thinking* or several variations of the concept can be traced back to the mid-20th century with relation to fields such as architecture and engineering. These were fields that were grappling with the digital revolution and a rapidly changing world (Dam & Teo, 2020). There is no clear way to trace the exact history of design thinking and its roots, as many academics have referenced design from various fields and ways of thinking about problems and how solutions are designed. While this chapter does not seek to offer a full and complete history of design thinking, there are a few individuals from various fields of study or professions worth noting as contributors to the idea.

In the 1960s, architect, futurist, and inventor Buckminster Fuller (1967) coined the term *design science*, taking scientific principles and applying them to solve human problems that he believed could not be solved by politics or economics. He focused on environmental sustainability and posited that individuals could be aligned to consciously making the finite planetary resources match their needs without causing damage or disruption to the ecology. Fuller called himself a comprehensive anticipatory design scientist, who was set on solving global problems and designing technology that could accomplish more with fewer resources (BFI Institute, n.d.). Fuller is considered by many to be one of the original thought leaders and contributors to design thinking.

In the late 1960s, psychologist and sociologist Herbert Simon (1969) discussed design as a method for a creative process that could transform current circumstances into preferable ones. Simon's work introduced the idea of design as both a mindset and a methodology. Simon also discussed the importance of bringing social sciences together around the idea of problem-solving. Simon shared that design has a series of steps, starting with problem definition, asking questions, generating ideas that could lead to a solution, and trying some of the ideas to choose the best one. Simon's work has since been criticized for neglecting some of the human factors essential in design, such as social interaction, intuition, and experience (Huppatz, 2015). Despite criticism, Simon's work served as a catalyst to many of the models of design thinking in use today.

In the 1970s, Horst Rittel, then professor of the Science of Design at the University of California, Berkeley, coined the term *wicked problems* to explain the complexity of problems designers seek to solve (Rittel & Webber, 1973). Additionally, Rittel looked at both design methods and design theory and created a link between design and politics. He emphasized the significance of the human perceptions and experiences in design. His work is highly regarded by many in the profession, and his work has made a tremendous impact on the field of computer programming and information science (Rith & Dubberly, 2007).

In the early 1980s, British educator and academic Nigel Cross (1982) argued that there needed to be a new path to education to complement the traditional paths of arts and humanities versus the sciences. He suggested that *design* (with a capital D), could be this path and defined it as "the collected experience of the material culture, and the collected body of experience, skill and understanding embodied in the arts of planning, inventing, making and doing" (p. 221). Cross noted that the conventional ways of knowing proposed by the humanities and the sciences neglected this third "designerly way of knowing" (p. 221), or the ways that designers think and create, the cognition behind design. Cross (1982) argued the need for design to become an academic discipline and an area of further research to bring understanding to the cognitive abilities required in design and how they can be developed through education. Cross continued to study designerly ways of knowing and in 2011 authored the book *Design Thinking: Understanding How Designers Think and Work* (2011), which provided insights and case studies in design thinking. His work continues to be celebrated in the field of design.

Later in the 1980s, philosopher and urban planner Donald Schön (1984) published his book *The Reflective Practitioner: How Professionals Think in Action*, which emphasized the importance of self-reflection to the design process and emphasized the importance of reflection-in-action. In that same decade, Peter Rowe (1987), who was then the director of Urban Design Programs at Harvard at the time, published a book entitled *Design Thinking*, which focused on the aspects of work of urban planners and architects. Through retelling of stories and case studies of approaches to design by planners and architects, Rowe argued that the common thread in design relates to inquiry or seeking out information that generates inspiration for creation.

The 1990s saw a rise in the popularity of design thinking. Management and design professor Richard Buchanan (1992) authored an article entitled "Wicked Problems in Design Thinking," in which he examined the origins of design thinking and drew on the work of Simon and Rittel to reopen an examination of wicked problems. In the same article, Buchanan drew a connection between design thinking and innovation and emphasized the interdisciplinarity of design in its application to many professions.

In 1991, the design firm IDEO formed from a merger of three parties: David Kelley Design, Moggridge Associates, and Matrix Product Design (IDEO Inc., 1994). IDEO coined the term *human-centered design thinking*, bringing together an interdisciplinary team of experts from various fields to facilitate design processes to design both products and services (Szczepanska, 2019). David Kelley, one of IDEO's founders, and his brother Tom Kelley, IDEO's general manager, are both considered to be experts and thought leaders in design thinking. In 2013, they coauthored *Creative Confidence:*

Unleashing the Creative Potential in Us All, a book that emphasized that creativity can be taught and design thinking is a method that facilitates the development of a creative mindset.

In 2005, Stanford University founded its d.school, bringing formal instruction to design and experiential learning and launching a fellowship in 2012 to partner with industry professionals and subject matter experts who have a design challenge, so that design could be taught applied through the lens of exploration and experimentation. Today, the Stanford d.school is known as the leading academic institute for design thinking (Whearley, 2017).

Thought Leaders in Design Thinking

Today, there are many well-known thought leaders in the design field. Much of their work has influenced the content that follows in this book. While this book is not intended to offer a full history and comprehensive examination of the design profession, the authors encourage readers who are keen to know more about design and its various applications to explore the multitude of modern work in the field. The following is a list that comes from IDEO of some of the experts whose work has helped inform modern design thinking practice:

- Shelley Goldman in K–12 education
- Roger Martin and Jeanne Liedtka in business
- Sarah Brooks in government
- Matteo Vignoli in food innovation
- Carl DiSalvo and Liz Sanders in design research, among others
- Antoinette Carroll, equity designer
- Terry Irwin, who researches translation design, a new area of design that encourages societal transition toward more sustainable futures— something akin to design thinking on a systems level

The same IDEO (2020b) list also cites a number of educational institutions who contribute to the research, curriculum, and resources used in design thinking, including:

- Berkeley Haas Innovation Lab
- Designmatters at Art Center College of Design
- Northwestern's Segal Design Institute

- School of Design and Creative Technologies at the University of Texas at Austin
- Stanford d.school
- MIT D-Lab

The authors are also aware that there is a growing list of institutions across the world using design thinking in interesting ways. There is a growing body of expertise in design thinking internationally. As the work continues to gain popularity, it is expected that the body of research and expertise will continue to grow.

3

DESIGN THINKING MODEL

Friday afternoons are team meeting times at the University of Toronto Innovation Hub. This is the time where several teams of four to eight students ranging from first-year undergraduates to upper-year PhD students gather together to complete their work. The energy in the room is high, and the respect that students have for one another is immediately evident. Some faces are laughing and smiling while others appear to be deep in thought. Some faces are perplexed. Looking around the room one can see that some of the groups have drawn mind maps and diagrams all over their whiteboards, while others are deep in conversation.

One team is working on writing their insights from student data on sticky notes from interviews and observations they conducted over the last several weeks about student experiences in study spaces on campus. Another team is having a heated debate over the order of phases in a journey map of the campus' classroom redesign consultation process on a prototype they are preparing for their meeting with their stakeholders next week. Yet another team is discussing the plan to facilitate conversation circles with students to gather information about mental health experiences in support of a campus-wide mental health task force. Some other teams of students are engaged in conversations, while others quietly draw their interpretations of data, and still others are role-playing prototyping scenarios of a front desk experience.

Throughout the room, these interdisciplinary teams of students are deeply engaged and involved in the meaningful and challenging work of design thinking. They are engaged in working on real campus issues and challenges that directly impact them. They have committed their work-study term to learning the process of design thinking and working collaboratively with others to apply these new skills to their assigned projects. This is a cocurricular experience for the students, and they will later describe the experience they gained in this term as having a substantial impact on their confidence levels and feelings of self-worth. They will also share that they developed many skills while engaged with the Innovation Hub—practical skills in design thinking, but also teamwork and presentation skills, the ability to problem-solve in different ways, and opportunities to bounce back from failure. They have a new mindset and approach to solving wicked problems in teams, and many of these students will go on to achieve tremendous career success upon graduation because of the experience.

As the leader of this project, I (Julia) look around this room and feel so proud of these students. I remember when I interviewed them. Some of them were so quiet and timid and had a hard time looking me in the eye. To watch these students come out of their shells and into who they really are is such a beautiful picture. I know that none of this is really about me—it is about the magic of a process that when carried out is so inspiring, it demands the best from people. It takes them out of their day-to-day routines and into a mindset that aligns with who they really are and works with their strengths. I am really here to offer support and guidance and encouragement and to challenge them to go deeper when they analyze the stories of their participants. Design teams always get uncomfortable in the data analysis because it is hard to find the root of the problem. Some people want to give up at this stage. In these moments I tell them that this is where the real work happens. This is the work that they are doing on behalf of the people who shared their stories. I remind them that the work is so important because it is how we honor and appreciate the stories entrusted to us, by finding the insights that they offer us. It is so uncomfortable because we can relate to each one of them as fellow humans, but we must do this work to honor them and to translate their stories into something that creates change.

The preceding brief glimpse into life at the University of Toronto Innovation Hub is offered here to illustrate that while design thinking is a process for innovation, it relies on a human-centered approach. Design thinking is actually a process that when carried out well looks a lot more like doing than thinking. More important, when teams of students, faculty, and/or staff gather together to engage in a design thinking process, it can be transformative. This transformation happens not only because innovative solutions that meet people's needs are developed, but because the people who engage with the process can be transformed by the learning and insight that design thinking and design doing offers.

Design Thinking Overview

The design thinking process has several stages: empathize, define, ideate, prototype, and test (Holcomb, 2020). In the following pages, each step is outlined and examples of its application are provided. This chapter is meant to serve as an overview of the design thinking process rather than a detailed how-to guide. Readers are encouraged to keep in mind that while design thinking is a process and a model, it is in the doing of design thinking where the real impact happens.

Some design thinking resources place a strong emphasis on the latter stages of design thinking, where solutions are designed. While it is tempting to jump to solutions, the earlier stages lay the foundation as they center empathy building, which generates valuable insights for true innovation as well as presenting an opportunity to gain deep understanding into the unmet needs of the population. When solutions are generated from a new understanding of needs, the innovations that design thinking begets, such as new programs, services, resources, and other outcomes, can have transformational impact.

Design thinking is an iterative process that continues over time to ensure that solutions generated are desirable to students and meet their needs, but also to ensure their feasibility and viability within the context where they are implemented. A design thinking process begins with a research question— something that loosely defines the problem to be solved or question to be answered. From there, the empathy and insight generation process allow the lived experiences of students to be documented through long-form interviews, observations, and other data collection methods. Once collected, the review and analysis of data commences to find themes and insights that allow for the creation of a point of view statement. To continue the process, the statement must be reframed into a question, known as a reframe question, used to inspire ideation (IDEO, 2015). Refining the original research question into a reframe question becomes the basis for brainstorming to generate radical ideas that answer the reframe question with potential solutions. Ideas from brainstorming are narrowed down and refined to the point where they can be prototyped and tested with students. Prototyping and testing generates additional data and feedback, providing an opportunity for iteration before the idea is implemented.

Planning for Design Thinking

Design Thinking Mindset

Design thinking is both a method and a mindset (IDEO, 2020a). Teams embarking on design thinking for the first time should be prepared for a mindset shift. At the Innovation Hub, design team members are encouraged to bring their own creativity and strengths into the process to shift out of a logical and linear way of thinking into a more creative mindset. There are no limits to the creativity the teams may use. For example, a design team of students looking at some stories of student mental health experiences on campus shifted into a creative mindset and chose to present their prototype in a creative way. The students created a large and multicolored brain using plasticine and overlaid it with 3D plasticine-created figurines and other artifacts to show actions that could be taken as potential solutions or ideas to address mental health on campus.

While many problem-solving mindsets encourage logical thinking, the design thinking process requires teams to navigate a great deal of ambiguity (Holliday, 2018). This represents a mindset shift away from traditional planning and assessment methods to a more unpredictable approach requiring creativity along with a willingness to discover new information through a different way of working. Design thinking asks teams to step into uncertainty where there are usually more questions than answers as new information unfolds. The structures within the process value and promote creativity and space for ambiguity, rather than a positivist scientific process where problems have clear answers. Exploring possibilities that understand and detangle wicked problems requires creativity, and creativity lives in the unknown.

There is comfort and stability in routine. Many institutions have worked hard to build structured institutional planning and assessment processes that have been done the same way for many years. The shift to working in this new way can feel like a daunting change. There may be an established organizational mindset around solving problems where solving problems is prioritized rather than the design thinking hallmark of a lengthy period of steeping in the problem to generate a deeper understanding and creating opportunities to reframe it. Design thinking requires designers to spend a substantial amount of time in the empathy phase examining the experiences of students deeply to better understand their needs. A common challenge is the ethic of problem-solving that permeates student affairs practitioner culture. The slow examination of problems can feel uncomfortable as the temptation to immediately find solutions creeps in (Design Thinkers Academy, 2018).

Wicked problems are complex and no one solution will fix the problem (Rittel & Webber, 1973). To be successful, designers must become comfortable sitting in the problem space and spending time to deeply understand the problem at many levels, from many perspectives, trying to get to some of the root causes of why things are the way they are. Staying with the problem often requires a mindset shift. Human nature primes designers to take an immediate leap to answers, which makes sense because human beings are problem-solvers by nature. Success requires intentionality to step outside one's natural comfort zone of solution generation and stay in the problem space long enough to build deep empathy for users and to ensure that the problem is well understood. While staying in the problem space sounds simple, it requires some unlearning to achieve.

Prereflection and Considerations for Design Thinking

It can be difficult to know where to start with design thinking, and an open mind when entering this process helps. A good starting point is the most fundamental concept in design thinking, which is designing *with* rather than *for* the end user (IDEO U, 2017). The idea to design *with* the end user rather than *for* them comes from the notion that people will use and/or support what they create. Design thinking allows the people who will be using the product or service to become active participants in the creation of the right solution, a powerful concept that is fundamental to the success of any project.

Equity and the Design Team—Who Should Be Part of the Team?

To truly design *with* people, an important question must be posed: Who should be part of the design team? For example, if the design project centers around students, it is essential that students become part of the team in some form. When forming the design team, there is an opportunity to think both strategically and intentionally about whose voices need to be heard, and whose participation would be beneficial. Marginalized and minoritized people and perspectives should be considered and they should be included in meaningful, not just symbolic ways. There are important power dynamics that exist when designing a solution. These must be acknowledged when bringing people into the process and approached with reflection so that participants can collectively strive to create more equitable spaces (Harrington, 2019). When engaging students in a design thinking process, it is important that institutions give consideration to appropriate compensation and/or reward for participation. The currency could be financial compensation for time spent, or perhaps course credit for an applied project, or some other reasonable and appropriate method of compensation.

On their web page, Creative Reaction Lab (2018), a community centered, youth-led design thinking practice, has created a design thinking process known as equity-centered community design, which combines the design thinking process with best practices from community development and equity work. This Equity-Centered Community Design (ECCD) process focuses on how design thinking can incorporate people, power, systems, actions, history, and healing into the design thinking process to dismantle systemic racism. ECCD centers the design team and asks them to consider who is a designer, what their role is, and to reflect on what they bring into the process. Creative Reaction Lab emphasizes humility in recognizing one's own biases as an important precursor to the empathy building process.

As previously stated, it is important to note that consideration should be given to how both design team members and those who participate in the process are compensated. Participating in a design team is a time and energy intensive process, and consideration to compensation and relief from other duties is important. Additionally, for folks participating in the process by being interviewed or asked to provide input, compensation can enable participation from those who may be otherwise unable to take part (Head, 2009). Offering appropriate compensation to design team members and participants is an important consideration.

Bias and the Design Team

All humans hold biases and the elimination of these from any design process is impossible. While bias cannot be eliminated, it is essential to raise awareness about the implicit and explicit biases held by individuals and the team as a collective. To ensure the design thinking process is approached from an equity and anti-oppressive lens, team members, both individually and collectively, must take time at the beginning of the process to share their identities, including places of power and privilege, and to name their biases. Once team members have been identified, each person must commit to reflecting on their opinions, biases, and experiences with the user population being addressed in the design process (Orensten & Rubin, 2018).

The process of bias identification can be likened to the bracketing process in the qualitative research method phenomenology, a philosophical method of inquiry to study, or rather unpack human experiences of a phenomenon (Soule & Freeman, 2019). Bracketing acknowledges that one's view of the world is biased by their experiences, and therefore suggests that one must peel away these individualistic views to get to the truth, similar to peeling back layers of an onion (Soule & Freeman, 2019). In equity-centered design thinking practices, there are clear parallels between the reflection on individual and team biases that takes place at the beginning, and bracketing. The following paragraphs offer some practical advice to identify and disrupt biases that is relatively easy to implement in a design process.

Facilitating conversations about bias is difficult and leaders of design processes are encouraged to take caution and bring in those who hold training and expertise in this area to help. To reflect on biases, or bracket, team members may wish to reflect and write responses to some important questions, such as the following which come from the practices of the University of Toronto (2020a) Innovation Hub:

- What is my personal experience with this population or issue?
- What thoughts come to mind when I think about my past and present interactions with this population or issue?
- Have I established my own set of truths about this population or issue (another way of thinking about this is to reflect on the things that one might say about the user group, or the stories that they tend to tell others about them)?
- Do I have certain biases, whether positive, negative, or neutral, about this population or issue?
- Considering all of this, are there people missing from this team? Who else needs to be included in this work?

Questions like these aim to help team members intentionally raise awareness about their thoughts and feelings and offer a common space for discussion around these issues. Other questions may be more appropriate in other contexts, and journal reflection based on a question is just one way to engage the team in this process.

Following the example of questioning as a tool for bias reflection, individual team members would benefit from a written recording of their responses to questions like these at the beginning of the process, and for the team to collectively discuss their learnings from doing so. These biases can be revisited and expanded throughout the process as new information and/or learning happens both individually and collectively. Although one's own opinions and thought patterns about users cannot be erased or eliminated from the process, taking time to do this reflection, and returning to it throughout, will keep it top of mind. The bracketing process means to suspend judgment about the experience, facilitating intentional analysis of the phenomenon of the experience by peeling away individual meaning-making until the only thing left is the experience itself (Vagle, 2018).

Design team members may also wish to share some of their reflections with others as an accountability plan, giving permission to one another to pay attention to areas where bias may be arising in the process and bringing reflections up as necessary with each other. It may be helpful for the team to have a list of these assumptions on a whiteboard or shared document to review them periodically throughout the design process.

Examining Other Data to Understand What Is Already Known

While the data collection for the design thinking process is largely qualitative, reflecting on other data sources such as surveys, metrics, and other quantitative data will support the process, particularly when it comes to defining a problem statement. As teams establish a question or problem they wish to answer or solve using design thinking, they should ask: What do we already know about this issue? What existing data and information exists? Exploration could include a literature review of current research around the topic at hand or a scan of institutional data. Securing as much information prior to moving forward with a design thinking process will be incredibly helpful to the process and can reduce how much new information needs to be collected. Prioritizing data collection mirrors best practices within student affairs assessment to never collect data that already exists somewhere else. Triangulation of existing data and research will support the team in reducing their cognitive load through the process, and help create more robust final outcomes that consider other reliable sources of information (Laferriere et al., 2019).

There are additional benefits to a robust preliminary assessment of existing data and information. A thorough investigation of what is already known will also support the design team in securing buy-in from other institutional partners and project stakeholders who may be skeptical about or unfamiliar with the methodology. Design thinking does not replace other forms of research and data collection. In fact, the process works best when it is used as one method in a complete toolbox of approaches.

One circumstance where examining existing data proved particularly useful was in the spring/summer of 2020 during the COVID-19 pandemic. Instructors and instructional support staff were incredibly overwhelmed by the rapid transition to online learning. At the University of Toronto Innovation Hub, a team working as part of the Transforming the Instructional Landscape initiative, a major learning space redesign project, had to work quickly to better understand the challenges faced by instructors during this time. Rather than collect primary data, the team realized that a vast amount of information was emerging in the media and in higher education journals and other publications. They swiftly conducted a literature review to gather as much useful information from these publications as possible, prior to planning to speak to instructors and support staff on campus. This work with existing research enabled the team to gain valuable information and insight into the challenges and make more efficient use of the time they had during interviews.

Drawing on Strengths: Team Expertise

As teams prepare to embark on the design process, the group should take time to learn about their team members' areas of expertise and skill sets, including background and experience in design thinking. In circumstances where the design thinking methodology is completely new to all team members, there may be opportunities to draw on other related experience from team members. For example, if engaging students who come from an academic background where they have engaged in ethnographic research, such as anthropology or sociology, there will be some parallels that can establish a shared understanding. Design thinking data collection methods are similar to ethnographic research, and engaging in a design process allows these students the opportunity to apply their well-honed academic research skills in a practical setting. As illustrated at the beginning of this chapter, a bonus to the design thinking approach is that the application of academic learning serves as an excellent work-integrated learning opportunity.

Team members may also discover a wide range of other useful skills in the group. Perhaps there are members who are extremely trustworthy and can put people at ease by building rapport in conversations. These skill sets are valuable when conducting participant interviews. Some may be the type who notice small details and appreciate nuanced beauty in the world. These team members will excel at participant observation. Others may be adept at critical thinking and analysis. These skills will be useful in data analysis and need finding. Are there members who excel at brainstorming and ideation and seem to always be coming up with new things? They may be highly creative and artistic or like to create visual representations of ideas. These individuals will be extremely helpful in the phases of the design process that require ideation and prototyping. Ultimately, a diverse range of skill sets will help a design thinking team tremendously, and taking time to identify these skill sets is time well spent.

Forming the Question

While it may seem simple, defining the problem that the design thinking process will endeavor to solve or the question it seeks to answer is a complex process. Arguably, problem definition, at the onset of the process and then during the refinement phase once insights are gathered, is the most important and most challenging part of this process. Feeling as though one already understands the problem through their own lens is natural, and believing that the answer to the question or solution to the problem is obvious or already known is tempting in most circumstances and spaces. In fact, jumping to conclusions and/or solutions rather than spending time gathering empathy for students and others involved in the matter to better understand their needs can often be the default approach. With rising challenges in many areas impacting the student experience, such as resilience and mental health, it is evident that there would be answers to important questions if this default approach was working, and existing solutions that are already addressing these unmet needs. If an institution has students who still face complex challenges, design thinking offers a different approach.

In design thinking, understanding the true nature of the problem one is trying to solve is crucial. This is why problem definition happens at two points in the process. Before data is collected in the insights phase, a general understanding of the issue or problem is needed. However, in design thinking the data shapes the problem definition, so there is another opportunity for problem definition that happens once the data is collected. Knowing the right questions to ask is a really important skill that is developed during design thinking.

Asking Great Questions

Successful design thinking requires asking the great questions. Design thinker Jorge Juan Perales (2020) argued that strong design thinking questions allow you to obtain the right type of information including the right quantity and quality of information. Perales went on to suggest a few characteristics of good design thinking questions. He stated that good design thinking questions:

- should empower and build trust;
- must challenge current assumptions and clarify issues;
- cause people to reflect, go beyond what is obvious and help people take things to the next level; and
- should open new possibilities and perspectives, encouraging breakthroughs in thinking.

Perales (2020) offers important considerations for question asking, which is foundational to the problem definition process. While the best design thinking questions can be stated simply, the multitude of potential answers are extremely complex. The complexity is where that problem definition happens.

In the initial stages of design thinking teams often have an idea of the issue or problem but lack important information to really define the problem. In particular, there is an issue, but the teams do not yet know what the unmet human needs are that would inspire a better option and inspire design. This is why asking good questions that generate stories is so important at this point in the process.

For example, a few years ago the Innovation Hub was asked to explore the experiences of students who are also parents on campus. At the time there was a general consensus within the U of T community that students who were also parents had many challenges, and that the university could do more to ensure that they were well-supported during their studies. They realized that what they wanted to know could be articulated in questions such as:

- What is life like for student parents? What does a typical day look like for them?
- What barriers and challenges and frustrations do they encounter in their lives as student parents?
- Are there resources on campus that are working particularly well to support them?
- Are there gaps in the resources available?
- How does it feel to be a student who is also a parent at U of T?

At this stage, the team took the original broad issue and narrowed it down into more specific, yet still general enough questions to give some scope to their task of inquiry. At this stage of the process, it makes sense for teams to collect some additional data and knowledge prior to moving on to directly speaking to participants.

Sources of Preexisting Information

As mentioned earlier, when exploring the initial question to answer or problem to solve, there are typically many data sources that are useful in expanding the understanding of the issue. Quantitative data such as institutional facts and figures, enrollment data, local and national survey results, and assessment data, for example, provide useful information. There may also be qualitative data from surveys, interviews, focus groups, and other reports or studies on the issue within the institution. Existing documents such as policies, web pages, and newspaper articles can also be considered existing data. Bringing together and reviewing all these existing data sources sets the stage for an effective design thinking process. An environmental scan of the issue is also incredibly useful. Questions for an environmental scan could include:

- Is this an issue or question that other institutions are facing?
- If so, what have they learned?
- Is there current academic literature on the topic?
- What does the research say that might be relevant?

Bringing together information about what is already known about the topic provides incredibly helpful framing for the process. In many cases, creating a summary briefing document or table containing relevant information and summarizing what is already known is advisable. Summary information will be extremely helpful to design team members during the process. In fact, if the design team is involved in bringing the information together, it will assist them to deepen their understanding of the issues.

When reviewing and compiling preexisting information design team members must pay attention to what information is still missing and what questions emerge from a thorough review of the data. Remember that there is a reason for embarking on design thinking—and often the reason is that despite already having a great deal of information, the problem or question persists, and the issue still poses a great challenge that requires an innovative solution. Often missing information surrounds questions about why we do things. In his bestselling book *Start With Why*, Simon Sinek (2009) explains that there is a tendency to look at what we are doing and how we are doing it rather than why. Sinek explains that the why speaks to the values and beliefs that people hold and what motivates them. The level of "why" is where design thinking seeks to understand students beyond what the data and literature suggest. The why gets into the stories of student experiences that highlight the values, beliefs, experiences, and needs that shape who they are and what motivates them. Deep information is what the design thinking team seeks to uncover in the process, and the existing information offers clues and questions that will serve as breadcrumbs for the team to follow as they embark on this journey. At this information gathering and review stage, teams should make note of questions that they would like to answer, other information that they find interesting and/or perplexing, and additional data that would assist the process. When several team members engage in this process, they can compare notes on their findings and better triangulate meaning.

Once outside information is gathered, analyzed, and synthesized, the team can come together to define the scope of the design thinking process and refine their questions based on new information. When discussing next steps, team members engage in a dialogue about their findings in reviewing preexisting data. The review could be done in a brainstorming session where each team member shares several questions and/or surprises they found when reviewing the data. Then new information can be compared, and the group can identify themes that they need to consider as they move into the empathy phase to collect data.

Empathy and Insight

The empathy phase of design thinking requires teams to participate in data gathering activities that will help them to better understand the mindsets of students. Empathy is a fundamental concept in design thinking whereby efforts are made to deeply understand the challenges and realities of the people for which the team is designing. Empathy can also be thought of as developing a deep understanding of the people who will benefit from the end design. The emphasis on building empathy and the amount of time spent on this task is one of the features of design thinking. The emphasis on empathy is comparable to phenomenological research which aims to understand the lived experience of someone regarding a specific phenomenon (Vagle, 2018). While an individual cannot fully experience things the way another person does, there are tools in design thinking that are intended to go beyond opinions and facts to the deeper experiences of individual participants. During the empathy phase, teams should aim to immerse themselves in the story and experience of the end user to find useful insights into the research question.

Empathy versus Sympathy

Empathy is a quest to understand the full spectrum of a person's experience: the good and the bad, the joy and the pain, the mundane, the choices and motivations in different contexts, and more (RSA, 2013). To truly empathize, a designer must feel with another person, and make attempts to go beyond understanding emotions, but to feel them in parallel to the extent that it is possible. Sympathy, in contrast, is understanding what a person is feeling, and often it implies that suffering is present. Designers carefully differentiate between empathy and sympathy and ensure that they make every attempt to fully experience the emotions and needs and wants of another to develop a vast understanding of their circumstances.

Empathy can be built through observation, engagement, and immersion (Battarbee et al., 2015). Designers observe how users interact with their environments, listening to what they say and observing their behaviors to gain insight into what they think and how they feel, looking for clues as to what they might need. They also engage with users directly through interviews and interaction with the goal of uncovering deeper insights into their beliefs and values. Finally, designers immerse themselves in the experience of their users, finding ways to emulate their environments or circumstances to attempt to gain a firsthand understanding of their experiences.

How Empathy Is Built

In design thinking, participant stories are gathered through interviewing, observations of both physical space and online data, and other methods that the design thinking team can create to build a deeper understanding of the population. Once data are collected using these methods, they can be analyzed to generate themes and insights, and will ultimately help to uncover user needs. This process does not mean to serve as research for publication, but rather information gathering to identify patterns in the data that may surprise or enlighten the design team, ultimately serving as inspiration to inspire ideas at a later phase of the process. However, data and evidence are still the basis for interpretation.

Learning From Extremes

The concept of an extreme user is employed in design thinking to ensure that people at either end of the spectrum of a defined group are considered in the design process so that the process is inclusive and equitable. Critical examination of the characteristics of the individuals on the margins of a given population creates empathy for the true problem at hand. Designers may find that needs and problems of users are amplified by focusing on the extremes (Mortensen, 2020b).

When discussing extremes, it is important to note that the concept of an average student or trying to design for a typical student is false and will not produce something new and innovative. Students are intersectional in their identities. Culture influences the ways in which people interpret the world around them, yet different cultures are often misaligned on their worldview. Colonialism works to keep a singular view of the world and this manifests in laws and other means of force in society, which therefore suppresses other worldviews, creating both discrimination and oppression (Bear, 2000). The design thinking approach to designing for extreme users suggests that the people whose identities may seem different from whatever the culture's view of a typical person is are incredibly valuable to the process and must be included in the generation of insights.

A designer must consider the full population of people that they will design for and understand the characteristics of the population through various lenses such as demographics, behaviors, and motivation. In design thinking at IDEO (2015), the organization suggests that a great deal of insight can be generated when a design team collects significant data from 10 extreme users in a population. While 10 individual experiences may not be statistically significant, if diversity of experience is considered when selecting participants, the extreme differences between individuals can offer stories that exaggerate or amplify the experience of other users. When themes and insights are generated among these extremely diverse participants, and saturation points are achieved, or common needs found, this information is incredibly valuable to the process.

The goal in finding extreme users is to look for those who have unique characteristics or qualities when compared to a general population. The point here is not to achieve a perfect definition or rule for extremes by categorizing students, but for the design team to have a robust discussion about what some of the thoughts and assumptions may be about people in this population, and what factors of experiences might exist in the nontraditional or deviant cases. When these discussions take place in advance of participant selection, the team can be aware of the range of experiences and factors that they might look for and where recruitment needs to take place. An awareness of the importance of extremes in design will help the team to be intentional with participant recruitment, ensuring diversity in participation even within a specific population. People are multidimensional and, especially when working with extremes, they play multiple roles across a variety of contexts in their lives.

Data Collection Methods

Design thinking offers creative methods and tools for collecting information about student experiences. Many of the tools have roots in ethnographic and phenomenological research and seek to deeply understand individual experiences. In a design thinking process, the team will need to employ several different types of data collection to fully understand student experiences. These methods aim to dive deep into individual stories and experiences. The importance is placed on rich, contextual, descriptive data that is transferable rather than generalizable. Empathy-based interviewing and participant observation are the most common data collection methods in this process, although there are emerging opportunities for collecting information that are discussed later in this chapter.

Interviewing

In design thinking, the goal of interviewing is to lead participants into a place of storytelling and conversation, rather than answering a series of specific questions. The intent is to create a conversational environment where the participant can be comfortable sharing their story with the interviewer. Interviews should provide an opportunity for the interviewer and interviewee to engage in an empathy-driven conversation in a confidential and safe setting. Questions are open-ended and probing questions are used to encourage participants to elaborate on details of their responses. Interviews can be time consuming, but they are one of the best ways to gather highly detailed and nuanced data about the user, their perspectives, needs, obstacles, motivations, and experiences (IDEO, 2015). Interviewers take a human-centered approach, making efforts to build rapport with their participants.

Interviews get to the core of the human experience. All persons who will be conducting interviews must undergo training in the interview process, as well as have a level of knowledge of equity principles and a sensitivity to the issues at play. In their book *Designing for Growth: A Design Thinking Tool Kit for Managers*, Jeanne Liedtka and Tim Oglivie (2011) emphasized important skills that interviewers must acquire including the ability to:

- put the interviewee at ease
- ask questions that lead to storytelling and compelling quotes
- maintain a posture of curiosity
- look for surprising data
- become comfortable with silence in between dialogue
- pay attention both in body language and tone of voice
- paraphrase without leading the interviewee
- listen for ways that the participant has modified their world that might give insight into unmet needs

The success of an interview depends largely on the skill of the interviewer, and training and practice in interviewing are essential to hone these skills.

Positioning members of the team with shared characteristics, attributes, and identities to those being interviewed in the interviewer's seat is valuable and should be done wherever possible. Creative Reaction Lab (2018) stressed that the communities and individuals who are affected by the problem or question in design research are experts in their own experiences and should be included on the design team. For example, a college looking to better understand the needs of their Indigenous student population would be wise to consider hiring Indigenous students and training them to conduct the interviews, rather than having staff interview students. When hiring Indigenous students and training them, their own knowledge of storytelling and its value to research design can be incorporated. Team members who do not self-identify as Indigenous can then support the process by setting up interviews or taking notes. The current example raises two important issues: power and similarity of identity. In having students conduct interviews with other students rather than staff, there is an attempt to create a more balanced power dynamic. When the students share a similar identity, the power is further balanced and the likelihood of creating a comfortable atmosphere for an open and honest dialogue between interviewer and interviewee increases.

Interviewing well requires planning, usually by creating an interview guide or protocol. The interview guide is helpful in the data collection phase to ensure that a relatively consistent approach to interviewing has been taken by all team members. The interview guide includes a script for interviewers and contains the information that will be shared with participants before the interview, the questions themselves, and the concluding information to be shared after the interview. Mortensen (2020a) stressed that the interview guide acts as a script where designers build questions that are tied to the goals of the project and what they would like to know. She emphasized that designers practice interviews with their guide to refine the questions, but also stated that going off-script at times to probe deeper into the story is appropriate in design thinking. For these reasons, interview guides are an important planning tool in the design thinking process, but they are not meant to strangle curiosity or instinct.

Coming back to the example of the Innovation Hub's inquiry into the lives of student parents, the team developed open-ended questions to ask student parents to help understand their lives. Questions were designed to elicit stories and get participants sharing in a free-flowing and narrative way. The following are the interview questions that the team asked during 1:1 conversations with student parents:

- Walk us through a day in your life.
- What resources, if any, do you access on campus to support you as a student with family responsibilities?
- In what ways, if any, do you feel like your experience is different from students who do not have family responsibilities?
- If you had the opportunity to give advice to a new student coming into their program who had similar responsibilities to you, what would you tell them?

These questions were designed in an open-ended way to build rapport with participants and to give the opportunity for data to emerge that they may not have thought to ask about and assess things that may be unknown. The questions are designed to open up all possibilities, while still being relevant to the main focus of the issue: how best to support students who are also parents.

Design thinking is most often considered research for the purpose of quality improvement or program design and may be exempt from ethics review processes; however, checking institutional guidelines for ethics policies and procedures and completing any steps required by these policies to ensure compliance is advised. As a best practice, even in cases of ethics review exemption, the team would be wise to implement some type of informed consent process for participants, so they are fully aware of the purpose of data collection and their rights in the process.

Consent, whether verbal or written, should offer participants full details about the design thinking project including goals, how the information obtained will be documented and stored, and how it will be used both short term and long term. Participants should feel they can withdraw consent at any time, even after the interview takes place, without penalty, and request to have any of their data destroyed. Difficult topics and experiences can sometimes come up during interviews, and participant physical and psychological safety is of paramount importance. Designers should always have a list of support resources at hand in case the data collection process negatively affects participants. Finally, participants should understand the timeline for the project and be aware of how the results or findings will be shared back with them once the project is complete. Building a strong rapport with interviewees is tremendously important, as they may play a critical role in the later stage of the design process, particularly regarding ideation and prototyping.

Effective interviewing is a developed skill that requires investment. An effective interview in the design thinking context might last anywhere from 25–30 minutes (Kwon et al., 2020) to an hour or more (Eines & Vatne, 2018), depending on the project, volume of information required, and the depth of conversation. The objective is to engage the participant in storytelling in a comfortable and safe environment where they can reveal their authentic experiences and opinions. A benefit to this approach is that it affords deep levels of engagement with each participant. With this level of depth, the interviewer can access information in a student's story that they could not otherwise access, information that speaks to the individual's needs and motivations.

In most cases, interviews are audio recorded and later transcribed for storage purposes. Tools that offer artificial intelligence transcription are useful for both audio and virtual interviews as they offer real-time transcription. Considerations for data retention must be taken in compliance with institutional privacy and accepted data storage guidelines. During the transcription process, any unique identifying details of the conversation should be removed in the interest of privacy and anonymity (Stuckey, 2014). The team may wish to discuss some guidelines around the de-identification process for their project, and what details will make sense to anonymize in their context. For example, often pseudonyms are used to protect the identity of participants when creating personas or when using quotations from data. Designers can offer participants to select their own pseudonym to empower and engage them. These anonymized interview transcripts are likely to become the primary source of data in the data analysis phase of the design thinking process. There are, however, other opportunities for additional data collection that should also be considered.

Observation

Observation of participants participating in day-to-day activities is a common data collection method in design thinking. Doing so enables design thinkers to learn about people's activities in their natural setting by observing and participating in those activities (De Munck & Sobo, 1998). During periods of observation, the design team visits spaces that participants frequent, engaging in activities that come naturally. The goal here is to look for patterns in activity and behavior and ways in which people modify their world that are interesting to note. For example, designers investigating a problem in student culture might visit a dining hall or common space to observe interactions and may notice patterns such as certain groups of students gathering, or certain students that appear isolated. When conducting observations, design teams should be careful about making generalizations based on individual observations, but rather look for trends and patterns in a larger data set of observation data.

The observer can take different stances in this method of data collection. In the participant as observer stance, the design thinker becomes a full participatory member of the group being studied whereby the group is aware of the participation of the observer. The participatory stance is the most immersive and allows for full experiential learning for the observer through participation. Another stance, the observer as participant, happens when the design thinker is in the same room as the group, identifies themselves as a researcher, has some social interaction with members of the group, but does not fully participate in its activities. Finally, the complete observer stance involves the design thinker taking a completely passive stance and can be either completely hidden from view or in plain sight where they are as unobtrusive as possible to the activities taking place (Zieman, 2012). Observation is an important data collection method as it allows the design team to immerse themselves in various ways with participants.

Depending on the situation or activity being observed, a different stance will be appropriate. For example, if the design thinker's goal is to better understand and observe a program designed to support students with their career endeavors, it may be beneficial that they take on the observer as participant stance to engage with the programming. In the observer as participant example, student team members are best positioned and most appropriate to take on the observer as participant stance. If staff also wish to observe, they could take a passive stance to avoid creating an awkward or uncomfortable power dynamic.

Documentation is an important part of observation, to ensure that the design team generates an adequate record of the data collected during these activities. Documentation for observation is collected in the form of field notes from the observer, or a detailed written description of the observations made, which can be done by creating jot or scratch notes, more detailed field notes, or a journal or diary (Emerson et al., 2001). Observers can also create more systematic guides or rubrics to be used in addition to or in place of the narrative field notes. Whatever method of data recording used, data must be promptly recorded and stored in a secure location.

To ensure the safety of all participants, ethical principles should be followed during observations. IDEO's *The Little Book of Design Research Ethics* (2016) offers four ethical guidelines for data collection that are designed to ensure participant safety. IDEO suggested that the team be introduced accurately without withholding any information and allowing the participants to ask questions and receive answers. The first guideline allows for participants to give informed consent. The second guideline instructs the team to listen empathetically without interjecting any advice or opinions. Participants should be able to express their viewpoints freely and openly. Third, the team is advised not to make promises to participants or set any expectations that might lead to disappointment. Finally, IDEO (2016) suggests that the design team take only the needed information about participants and respect them as people in the process. Respecting participants includes respecting their time and being mindful of any cultural sensitivities that might be at play. Taking an ethical approach ensures the integrity of the observation and preserves participant safety.

Other Data Collection Methods

There are other data collection methods in design thinking that can incorporate creativity to support building empathy for end users. While this book will not explore these methods in detail, there are a few that are worth mentioning here. The following examples are methods also used in design thinking as a form of data collection:

Immersive experiences. Immersive experiences are situations constructed by the design team with the goal of building empathy for users (Liedtka, 2018). A classic example of an immersive experience used in design for individuals who are blind or have a sight-related disability is to restrict the vision of a sighted person to varying levels and have them interact and engage with a physical space to simulate the experiences of the vision-limited person. These kinds of experiences are usually imperfect but allow the team to foster empathy without directly involving participants as a part of wider data collection efforts.

Digital ethnography. Digital ethnography or online data collection involves the design team reviewing publicly available online information to build empathy for users and gain insight into the design challenge subject matter (Pink, 2016). The digital ethnography method allows design teams to collect data using digital media artifacts rather than interacting with live participants. Increasingly, online spaces are places for discourse and dialogue in various channels that can offer interesting insights into deeper needs of a given population.

Group interviewing. Group interviewing involves hosting dialogue-based events where a group of end users or potential users discuss questions like those used in the interview process. These events offer the opportunity for new insights to emerge from dialogue among a diverse group of participants. Intentional choices based on principles of equity should be made when inviting participants to take part in group interviewing. Group interviewing ensures that the ensuing discussion includes diverse perspectives and a rich discussion (IDEO, 2015). Group interviewing is a great segue into other design thinking activities such as idea generation and cocreation sessions.

At the University of Toronto Innovation Hub, group interviewing is becoming a preferred method of data collection as it has unique benefits, especially when the interviewees are students. Innovation Hub teams have found that when groups of students come together to discuss their experiences on campus, they begin to realize that others share a common experience and/or challenge and they report that they feel better after having attended the group interview because they realize they are not alone. Innovation Hub teams have employed group interviewing in both in-person and online environments. When students are the participants, the Innovation Hub ensures that staff and/or faculty are not present in the physical or digital room as this provides a space for safer and more honest dialogue.

Taking inspiration from other areas. Taking inspiration from other areas involves comparing the design project or challenge to other challenges or problems that have similar elements but might be different. Taking inspiration is a form of observation where the team looks for successful designs in other areas that solve a similar problem to the design team's current challenge (IDEO, 2015). For example, a university that wishes to design spaces on campus that support student well-being can draw inspiration from other areas such as spas, health clinics, fitness centers, and office spaces that have been redesigned for employee well-being, among others. The idea here is that inspiration can be gained from areas that are seemingly unrelated to the design challenge, but at a deeper level speak to some of the implied user needs.

Design thinking is a creative process and therefore there are few limits on how the team can think about the best opportunities to build empathy for the population they intend to design for. Provided that these data collection methods are carried out in an ethical way and consider potential equity issues, the team can explore creative ways to design a unique data collection process using multiple methods. It is important that the design team find ways to connect back with participants and share their learnings and summarize findings. This transparency in sharing back data is a good moment to check in with participants to ensure their information was documented correctly and to see if they have anything to add.

Data Analysis

In design thinking, teams collect a large amount of qualitative data that will be analyzed to generate themes and insights about student needs. Beginning the data analysis phase is a good opportunity for each team member to read through all the interview transcripts and field notes and reflect upon documentation of any additional data collection that took place. At this point it is also helpful for team members to reread any bracketing notes or memos they made when reflecting on their biases at the beginning of the process to reintroduce this awareness when looking at the data.

Generally, data analysis is best done using a hybrid approach of individual team members reviewing data, combined with the team members coming together in dialogue around what they are seeing and the themes that are coming together. At this time, there may be secondary research that could be useful in the data analysis process. Some design thinking teams may wish to explore academic literature and other sources related to the design question. If this was done prior to the data collection, the data analysis stage is a good chance for the team to review the secondary research that was completed. Essentially, the team will benefit from coming together and reviewing what was known about the design problem or challenge prior to the data collection.

Needs Finding—Generating Themes and Insights

In student affairs, students may be involved in program design processes through questioning them about what they want and need. This can fail to generate truly meaningful solutions because it relies on a high level of self-awareness and competency among students involved, which developmentally is not always the case. The design thinking process is ultimately about uncovering deep needs of users, beyond stated needs, into the deeper unmet needs revealed through the empathy building process. Doing so will change the direction of decisions that come next. The goal of data analysis is to uncover the broad themes around user needs found in the research and the more specific insights that provide evidence for each theme. In design thinking, there are many ways to analyze data. When there is a large amount of data, coding the data systematically is one of the most methodical ways to approach this task. Books that offer in-depth instruction for coding such as Saldaña's *The Coding Manual for Qualitative Researchers* (2015) or Moustakas's *Phenomenological Research Methods* (1994) are highly regarded resources for teams as they embark on this process.

Generally, in design thinking, teams will take time to read through and reflect on all the data prior to coding and then begin an open coding process, reading for broad themes. Once the broad themes are identified through open coding, the team members can come together and use discussion or sticky note sessions to narrow down the information into well-articulated themes. In design thinking, group energy supports the data analysis process as team members discuss and share moments during data collection that they found particularly compelling or interesting, forming a collectively con-structed narrative. For example, perhaps there was something in the data that a team member found surprising, or maybe upsetting. These moments are the insights—or ah-ha moments—that are so meaningful and important to explore further and spark deeper dialogue. The team often can use its collec-tive intuition to uncover some of the most powerful insights through group dialogue and sharing.

There are many tools and methods offered in design thinking that support data analysis. One of the most used methods is known as empathy mapping. In this process, the team looks at the data through four lenses: what people said, did, thought, and felt (Kelley, 2018). Determining what was said in interviews is relatively simple, and what they did by observa-tion is also straightforward, but looking at thoughts and feelings is more abstract and requires inferences to be made. These can come from other cues at times, such as people's body language, or their reactions to different experiences noted in the data. Tools like empathy mapping provide support to the design thinking in the analysis phase that offer a concrete task to do with data that is abstract. Considering the analysis methods that will be used prior to data collection is critical to ensuring that the correct type of information can be obtained.

Data analysis takes time and can bring about tension as team members may each view the information through a slightly different lens. While some themes and insights emerge quickly with team consensus, others may require debate and dialogue as some data points may be contradictory to others. Ultimately, the design team learns and grows through this process of deep analysis, and once the final agreement is made with regard to themes and insights about user needs, the team can take those back to the participants to receive commentary. The remainder of the design process, particularly the prototyping and testing phases, will be invaluable feedback for the team as to the accuracy of their interpretation of the data. These phases rely on a well-defined problem, reframed in a point of view statement generated from the data.

Defining the Problem

Defining the real problem that the team is trying to solve in the design thinking process is a complex process. Recall the discussion about mental models earlier. These mental models, or the lens through which individuals see the world, are what makes problem definition so challenging (Hester et al., 2012). Each person has an inherent set of biases and worldview or paradigm that acts as a lens through which they filter new information. These mental models are what help us understand the world, quickly solve problems, or apply reasoning to new information (Hester et al., 2012). Essentially, mental models help the brain to process a vast amount of information in a logical and timely way so that people can function in the world. While there are many benefits of mental models, they still come with some limitations because, as they are affected by societal systems of power and oppression, they support individual biases, and it is critical to be aware of this connection.

Problem definition requires more intentional and conscious thinking and more careful information evaluation. Recall the earlier discussion on Daniel Khaneman's modes of thinking in chapter 1. Whereas System 1 thinking is fast, emotional, and based on instinct, problem definition requires a slower and more concerted thinking process where the brain can become more aware of potential gaps in thinking and biases using System 2 thinking, a more deliberate and slower thought. When compared to the automatic thinking that happens quickly using System 1, moving intentionally into System 2 thinking throughout the design thinking process can help avoid jumping to conclusions or what Kahneman (2011) calls WYSIATI (what you see is all there is) and allows for more intentional and critical thought.

In the example of students who are also parents, the team's interview process yielded some interesting data. One of the key findings was that student parents were hungry to find belonging on campus, and much of that came down to being more visible. Essentially, the team learned that so many of the university's policies and practices were not family friendly. They were looking to be more recognized and visible on campus. This insight was critical to the team's ability to reframe the problem into a point of view statement.

The Point of View Statement

As was mentioned earlier in the chapter, the most important and complex part of the data analysis process is problem definition. The team uses the data collected in the empathy phase of the process to create a point of view statement, or an actionable statement of the problem which is generated based on the data collected in the empathy phase (Dam & Siang, 2019b). The point of view statement emphasizes the discovered user needs that were collected in interviews and observations and other data collection methods. From there the point of view statement is converted to an actionable problem statement that will guide the remainder of the design process. The point of view statement works to guide the team moving forward and becomes instructive in the ideation phase. While this may seem simple, problem definition is quite challenging because of the many ways that individual team members may see the problem. Teams that fail to pay attention to defining the problem effectively may struggle with a lack of clarity or working at cross-purposes as they embark on the next phases (Jacoby, 2017).

In the example of student parents at the University of Toronto, the information about students' need for visibility as parents was reframed into the following questions: *How might the University of Toronto intentionally increase the visibility of students with family responsibilities? How might the university's spaces become more family friendly and welcoming of student parents?* These questions offered more definition to the problem that student parents were really facing on campus: They felt invisible. Once the problem was put into this reframe, the design process had its inspiration to move forward and think about ideas for solutions. The ideation processes and outcomes for this project are discussed later in the chapter.

Another example of a reframe or a *how might we . . .* question from the University of Toronto (2020b) Innovation Hub came from a partnership with the campus's Multi-Faith Centre, which supports spiritual wellness of those on campus and gives opportunities for people to explore questions of purpose, meaning, and identity together. The center partnered with the Innovation Hub with the goal of redesigning its programs to better meet student needs. The design process included students from all faith backgrounds, including students who did not identify as having a particular faith or belief system.

In the review of the data and in discussions with the staff at the Multi-Faith Centre, the impact of these programs was identified as helping students with meaning-making and/or understanding the context of their experiences within the bigger picture of their life and the world. The Multi-Faith Centre wanted to understand how they could meet the spiritual needs of all students in their search for meaning, purpose, and identity in everyday life. The question was broad enough that it allowed infinite possible answers and/or solutions but defined the scope of the engagement and gave focus for the conversations that the team would have with students.

Embarking on a design process with this question allowed the Innovation Hub team to have productive conversations with students in the research phase, and they were later able to refine the design question in much more specific terms using insights from the data they gathered. The insights phase revealed that for the students interviewed, faith helped students to find community and belonging, a sense of purpose, and supported positive emotional experiences. Further, they learned that faith offered students a framework for understanding the world. In this case, the *how might we . . .* or reframe questions became those of exploring possibilities to recreate these experiences. Several reframe questions emerged, such as:

- How might the Multi-Faith Centre design programs that offer the opportunity for students to explore new ways to understand the world?
- How might the Multi-Faith Centre ensure that their services support building a sense of community and belonging in students?
- How might the Multi-Faith Centre hold space for students to process emotional experiences in a supported way?

The data allowed for numerous reframe questions to be developed that added scope to the original question.

Some design experts believe that it is important for the team to spend most of the time in the design process working with and exploring the problem, and a far lesser amount of time ideating solutions. Albert Einstein was known to have said that if he had an hour to solve a problem, he would think about the problem for 55 minutes and spend only 5 minutes actually solving the problem (Spector, 2016). The success of design thinking projects rests on the team's ability to define the real problem behind challenges that were identified at the beginning of the project based on collected data. Design teams are urged to take their time in the data analysis and problem definition phases of the process.

The point of view statement is a concise way for the design team to capture the problem in a way that includes the user characteristics with the needs identified in the empathy phase of data collection and the insights generated in the data analysis process. Point of view statements should be written in a compelling way to be effective in clearly articulating the problem and how it impacts the end user (Dam & Siang, 2019b).

Another example of a point of view statement might be as follows: *Commuter students often travel over 1 hour per day and need rest and connection with others that nurture their feelings of belonging on campus.* In this example, the statement is structured where the phrase *commuter students often travel over 1 hour per day* is the user description, the needs are defined as *rest and connection with others* that came from an insight that commuter students often lack feelings of belonging on campus. The previous statement clearly and succinctly expresses the design team's task by defining the user, their needs, and the problem they face.

Once a compelling point of view statement is generated, the team can reframe the statement into a question. In design thinking, the phrase *how might we . . .* is often used at the beginning of these questions. The purpose of the new question is to fuel the ideation phase of the design process. Using the commuter student challenge as an example, the problem statement can be reframed with a question. In this case, the question could be reframed as follows: *How might we design opportunities for rest and connection with others for commuter students that meet their need for a sense of belonging?* A good test to ensure that the reframe question has been written effectively is to confirm that there could be many possible answers to the question. In this example, there could be many ways to design opportunities for rest and connection on campus; thus the problem is reframed into a question that can be used to ideate possible solutions.

Generating Goals and Outcomes

With a well-defined problem, a strong point of view statement, and a clear reframe question, the team is almost ready to proceed to the ideation stage of design thinking. Almost, but not yet. Many teams find value in taking a moment to pause and look at goals and design constraints to guide ideation. IDEO (2020a) explains that innovation happens at the intersection of desirability—a solution that is desirable to the user that will actually meet their need, a feasible solution that can be implemented within current organizational operations, and viability—a solution that can be sustained over the long term. The desirability, feasibility, and viability model help evaluate solutions.

The team may also wish to review the point of view statement and think about identifying design constraints, such as budget, timelines, or any other restrictions or limitations that they should impose on ideas to ensure that the needs of users and the institution will be met. The practice of imposing constraints preemptively can also ensure that the idea has a chance at successful implementation.

Data as Inspiration and Influence

There are many ways to share data in a design thinking process. Decisions about how to do so should be based on the audience targets and why they need to know the information that was gathered. In some cases, the design team will only need to share information internally for the purpose of inspiring ideation and prototyping. In other projects there may be numerous stakeholders who wish to learn about the needs identified in the insights gathering phase. The design team has a responsibility to ensure that data is presented ethically and with integrity. When the team captures people's experiences, there is a correlated responsibility to share them honestly and with integrity to decision makers and stakeholders who have the power to influence change and support potential solutions. To determine the best option for data presentation, the team might want to consider a few guiding questions, such as:

- Who needs to receive this information and why?
- Are there people who could be consulted or brought in at this phase who can influence actions or change in the areas identified?
- How much information should be shared?
- What might be the best format for information sharing?
- What are the implications for sharing the data? What considerations or precautions need to be taken?
- Who else might this information be passed onto in the future? What considerations need to be made for secondary and tertiary receivers of the data?

The data collected during the insights phase of the design thinking process can easily be translated into influential storytelling material.

Data from a design thinking insights process can be presented in different ways. Some teams choose to do this informally through dialogue, while others will build reports and presentations to thoroughly document what was learned. Often, the data collected for one design project might have implications for other projects or questions. The data may even shed light on issues that matter to others that the team might not have anticipated. Sharing data is also an opportunity to consider inviting others into the process whose perspectives may be useful in the ideation and prototyping phases.

Ideation

Collecting stories of human experiences builds deep empathy for the population being focused on and the result is inspiration. Inspiration becomes fuel for idea generation in the ideation process. Ideation is a creative process where teams generate new possibilities to solve a problem or meet a challenge. The earlier phases of design thinking differentiate ideation from regular brainstorming because this phase now has better definition based on deeper insights into human experiences corresponding to that issue. The ideation process incorporates both individual reflection as well as group processes, such as brainstorming and discussion with diverse team members, and focuses the team on working together to collectively share energy and generate new possibilities. There are many methods of ideation that are highly creative. Occasionally, others beyond the design team are invited to join this process to ensure that all stakeholder perspectives are captured. Engaging in design thinking structured ideation generates solutions that are more innovative than the most obvious solutions (Dam & Siang, 2020b). The goal of the ideation phase is to put all of the possibilities on the table, even the most radical, and narrow them down into those that the team feels are best to prototype and test.

Preparing for the Ideation Phase

Ideation is an exciting phase of the design thinking process and often teams enjoy spending time generating ideas to solve problems or challenges that are now better understood. To ideate well, teams may wish to do some preparatory work so that they can make the best use of their time together. Preparatory work is particularly important when teams choose to invite other participants into the process. The best preparation for ideation is to ensure that there is a well-formed point of view statement, and a number of strong *how might we . . .* questions to work with when brainstorming that are neither too narrow, nor too broad (Dam & Siang, 2020b). The best questions are refined enough to offer a multitude of possible answers, but not so broad that the team will lack focus when generating ideas.

Some teams may wish to prepare by conducting secondary research about the problem or issue identified in the point of view statement before ideation takes place. In their book *Universal Methods of Design: 100 Ways to Research Complex Problems, Develop Innovative Ideas, and Design Effective Solutions,* Hanington and Martin (2012) emphasized that secondary research, sometimes known as desk research, can help the design team to understand the information that already exists on the topic and where there are gaps in the information which present opportunities for new designs. It also helps the design team to better define the scope of their project, and therefore the focus of the ideation session. Secondary research involves collecting and sourcing information from existing data including research papers, journals, books, conference materials, statistics or readily available quantitative data, white papers, online articles, opinion pieces, and other sources which can be summarized in a literature review (Hanington & Martin, 2012). Once teams have read all the information generated in both primary and secondary research, they are well-equipped to generate innovative ideas.

Equipped with a series of *how might we . . .* questions and a better understanding of the issue based on secondary research, the design team is ready to brainstorm. Dam and Siang (2020b) argued that team members need to intentionally adopt several characteristics in order to brainstorm well, which include:

- the ability to adapt how they see and understand the problem as new information and input emerges in the process;
- connecting concepts and themes that seem unrelated to create new possibilities;
- willingness to disrupt commonly accepted assumptions, beliefs, and norms and rethink traditional approaches;
- turning roadblocks into opportunities by changing directions or flipping them;
- the creative ability to visualize a new reality by dreaming and imagining new possibilities;
- using curiosity and experimentation to take risks and venture into the unknown;
- bringing together common threads to recognize patterns and make new meaning of information to build solutions; and
- finding comfort in being uncomfortable and using curiosity to ask crazy questions.

By striving to embody these characteristics during the ideation process, the team will be better equipped with a mindset and disposition that fuels the creativity required to generate new possibilities.

Teams may also wish to plan their ideation sessions to ensure that there are constraints governing how much time will be spent on each activity and thought given in advance to facilitation logistics. This might include who will facilitate the session and how the facilitator will support the group in developing the mindset required for ideation. The choice of facilitator will influence the quality of ideation, and a strong and well-prepared facilitator will set the tone for the session. Teams can then set goals for each session in advance and create a plan for how those goals will be met. Choosing activities that are appropriate for the topic and goals should follow as another important part of the preparation (IDEO U, 2020). Fun is an important part of ideation, and planning activities such as an energizing warm-up activity or icebreaker can help set the tone for the session.

Ideation Methods

The internet is rife with ideas and methods that can be used in ideation processes. Many of these methods are similar and all encourage creativity. The following section will highlight some of the common features of ideation methods and mention some resources to find others. While not an instructional guide for ideation, it will offer suggestions for further exploration of the topic and act as a good starting point. Design teams should strive to match their ideation method to the question or challenge that they are exploring as identified in the point of view statement.

Generally, some form of brainstorming is a preferred method for ideation. To prepare for a brainstorming session, a facilitator can be identified and ground rules for brainstorming chosen. IDEO's brainstorming rules include:

- defer judgment
- encourage wild ideas
- build on the ideas of others
- stay focused on the topic
- one conversation at a time
- be visual
- go for quantity (IDEO U, 2020)

These rules allow for individual creativity in a brainstorming session while ensuring that respect for team members happens at this time. Often, in brainstorming sessions, a "yes . . . and" approach is encouraged to build on ideas. For example, rather than disagree with someone's idea, team members are encouraged to use the phrase "yes . . . and . . . " to build or pivot on the idea previously presented (MSG, 2020). The team of design thinkers should focus on generating many ideas rather than thinking about practicality at this point. In fact, radical and wild ideas can help to guide the team's thinking into a more realistic idea that may not have been identified. There should be guidelines around brainstorming and throughout the ideation phase to ensure that the team can work together respectfully, while continuing to fuel the creativity required for innovation.

As previously mentioned, there are many ways to ideate, such as brainstorming, and numerous resources from which to draw inspiration. IDEO's publication entitled *The Field Guide to Human Centered Design* (2015) contains over 20 methods for ideation that are commonly used by design teams which include those that are variations on traditional brainstorming. Additionally, the Board of Innovation (2019) summarized their favorite tools for ideation including methods such as analogy thinking, where an idea from another area is translated to the problem at hand, to generating new ideas. An example of how a problem was addressed in the health-care industry could be translated into inspiration for how to address an education-related problem. Another example they shared was a round-robin method where ideas are written on sticky notes by each team member and passed around a circle for feedback. Another excellent resource is a list provided by Innovation Management detailing their seven greatest ideation techniques which includes methods such as generating wishes about the outcome and then using ideation as a way to help them come true (Frey, 2020). These resources are just some of the many which speak to methods for idea generation. They also include information on specific ways that teams can refine their ideas and prepare to select the most appropriate ideas for prototyping, which is the next phase of the design thinking process.

Recall the example of the Innovation Hub's work with students who are also parents. During this project, it was impossible to have student parents as part of the design team because while efforts were made to recruit their participation as team members, student parents were so busy with school, family, and other responsibilities that they were not able to be part of the team. The team consisted of students who were not parents working on a design process in consultation with student parents. In this case, ideation was done in an event format. In the summer after the initial insights from the insights phase showed that student parents needed to be visible on campus, the team hosted an ideation event. During this event, hosted at the Robarts Library family friendly study space with organized activities for children, student parent participants were presented with information about the key findings from the original research and engaged in a series of ideation events as a group.

Participants were asked to ideate in three ways. The first was a discussion-based activity using the question: *What simple things can U of T do to be more family friendly?* During this session, the group shared their ideas around practical ideas to answer the question. Next was the creative activity where the student parent participants were asked to draw a picture of a family friendly space that was not intentionally designed for families, then discussed the elements and principles that they considered essential for a family friendly space. Finally, the participants engaged in a role-playing activity where they role-played a scenario that they encountered as student parents and brainstormed possible solutions, with the benefits and drawbacks for each. All of these activities led to a tremendous number of ideas being generated that the team was able to compile. An idea that was particularly compelling was for the university to host a conference that focused on making higher education family friendly. This idea was carried forward into the prototyping stage and will be discussed later in the chapter.

Ideation is a fun and engaging part of the design thinking process that allows ideas to be generated to solve the problem or challenge. There are numerous methods to generating these ideas, all of which encourage creativity. The ultimate goal with ideation is to have a wide variety of practical ideas that can be carried forward into the prototyping and testing phases.

Prototyping and Testing

When teams have settled on some solution ideas, they are ready to begin prototyping and testing. There is no defined transition point into these phases because ideation, prototyping, and testing are often cyclical phases of the design thinking process that repeat as new information emerges. Prototypes are physical artifacts that represent an idea, complex and dynamic in nature, used as active tools to make decisions in the design process (Lauff et al., 2018). The purpose of a prototype is to provide a tangible artifact to potential users of the idea or solution to generate honest feedback and observations about how they actually use the solution and compare that information to what the team originally expected or intended in the ideation phase.

Prototypes can be physical models, drawings, storyboards, or even conversations or role-plays. There are numerous methods to prototype an idea, depending on the nature of the idea, but the important thing is that a prototype brings the idea to life such that it can be experienced and/or interacted with amid group of people from the end user population. When prototyping and testing, design teams aim to generate the artifact or concept as quickly as possible with minimal effort such that they can present it to their stakeholders for feedback. The prototyping and testing process acknowledges that people are highly visual and experiential and provides the opportunity to present ideas to people in a way that they can engage and interact with them where the team can see obstacles and/or challenges that may not have come up in the ideation phase (Donati & Vignoli, 2015). The concept becomes tangible in some way for the purpose of interaction and testing by users and eventually refinement by the team.

A great example of prototyping and testing comes from I-Think, which readers will remember from earlier in the book as a nonprofit making real-world problem-solving core to every classroom. A different year, students in Rahim Essabhai's class at John Polanyi Collegiate Institute were given the opportunity to consult with the food bank—that was renting space in the school—to improve the user experience. In this case, the food bank told students that their clients were asking them to change aspects of their operations. For example, they wanted the way that food was sorted to be changed to better reflect dietary restrictions.

The students embarked on the insights phase and gathered data through interviews and observations in the space. A particularly impactful moment in the insights phase was the story of one of the students in the class conducting the inquiry named Colin. Colin recalled an experience of his own mother walking to the food bank. He saw his mom, a woman who he had always regarded as powerful and well-respected, looking down at the floor as she walked to the food bank. He realized that there was a disconnect between how he viewed his mother and how she was in the moment. The team collected other data during the insights phase such as observing that clients spoke a variety of languages and, with a website only in English, information online about the food bank was inaccessible to some. Additionally, clients had to stand outside waiting in the cold due to the small size of the space. They also found that clients could not find the space easily as it was located at the back of the school with a door from the parking lot, which meant that they often had to go to the school office to ask for instructions on how to find the food bank. All of this data led the student team to reframe the challenge into an issue of dignity. They created a reframe question: *How might we design food bank experiences that allow people to retain their dignity?*

With this reframe question, students were able to generate numerous prototypes for testing. They narrowed many ideas down into three prototypes to test with stakeholders. The first was a recommendation to translate the food bank's website into multiple languages that were spoken in the community. Because the food bank had many volunteers from the community who spoke these languages, they were able to implement this solution quickly and observed that more people could access the information needed. The second solution was to make the signage clear by adding arrow stickers so that clients could make their own way to the food bank entrance. This signage worked by reducing the number of inquiries in the office and was adopted as well.

The final recommendation presented was that the food bank should purchase and install an awning and picnic tables for the waiting space outside of the food bank. The client loved this idea, but when they looked at pricing, they realized it was not feasible and/or viable for them at the time, but it helped them to think about the design of a new space, which was planned for in the following 2 years. As illustrated by the preceding example, prototyping is a practical approach to solution testing that allows design teams to test theories about what might work in a low stakes way. The I-Think food bank example illustrates this well.

Minimum Viable Product

In his book *Lean Startup,* Eric Ries (2011) introduced the concept of a minimum viable product (MVP). An MVP is a prototype or representation of an idea that the team can create with minimal effort and resources that will help prospective users gain a full understanding of the idea and provide feedback. Prototypes or MVPs can be physical representations of an actual product, digital representations of a software or technology-based solution, or experience-based representations of a service or experiential idea (Dam & Siang, 2019a). The nature of the idea will dictate the type of prototype required. For example, if prototyping a smartphone app, the prototype may be a series of drawings of what the user interface of the app would look like on the phone, and the series of screens that the user would encounter. The smartphone app example is quite different from prototyping a front desk experience, which might look like a series of role-play conversations with potential users that could gauge their reactions to different approaches.

Learning from failure acts as a catalyst during the prototyping and testing phases of design thinking. Teams aim to fail to generate the learning that fuels refinements and improvements to their solution. The famous Thomas Edison phrase "fail fast, fail often" is commonly used in design thinking to emphasize this important concept. While designing the lightbulb, Thomas Edison apparently failed more than 9,000 times before he completed his successful invention (Pontefract, 2018). The importance of the fail fast, fail often concept is that the learnings from failure be used as the creative fuel to drive innovation and change, allowing teams to use it to build upon and change original ideas to make them more relevant to the needs of the population for whom they are designing (Pontefract, 2018). Teams can then translate the learning into adjustments in the next version of their idea or solution.

Considerations in Prototyping and Testing

When embarking on the creation of a prototype or MVP, the team must consider four key areas: people—the users the prototype is intended to be used by, objects—the item or product itself, location—where the prototype will be implemented, and interaction—the experience that is envisioned by the team (Dam & Siang, 2020a). As these questions are answered the team can decide on methods of prototyping. In physical prototyping, a physical representation of the item can be built with low cost materials that show the potential. Physical prototypes should be created as scrappy, not crappy, representations of the envisioned final product (Godin, 2019).

Digital prototypes can often be created without designing an app or software solution. Sometimes a paper-based drawing of possible user interface screens is enough to generate initial feedback from users. For experiences, role-playing, journey mapping, or storyboarding can be used to represent the idea in a way that can generate feedback. There are truly no limits to the methods for prototyping. The team may only be limited by their imagination and available resources. The idea is to generate the prototype early to solicit feedback such that changes can be made and new prototypes generated to elicit more feedback.

Feedback Management

In design thinking, feedback has many uses. It helps the team to refine prototypes, but it can also bring them back to the empathy phase as they learn more about their users in the process. In some cases, feedback can even drive the team to refine their insights and adjust the point of view statement and reframe the question. Feedback is an essential part of the design thinking process as it enables the team to iterate on their ideas to ensure that the final design is desirable to the user. In the feedback process, the team should generate user feedback on the prototype itself, but also solicit other stakeholder feedback from people who also have a stake in the final design. These stakeholders can offer important feedback that speaks to the feasibility and viability of the prototype as a potential solution. In design thinking, the goal of testing prototypes is to generate as much feedback as possible that can be channeled back into future iterations. The team may wish to create a system to collect and document feedback.

There are several ways to generate feedback. Of course, listening to users and other stakeholders discuss their thoughts about a prototype is incredibly valuable, and allowing them to offer suggestions for how it can be improved can be insightful as well. There is also an opportunity for observation, to watch how the end users interact with the prototype. Based on their reactions and interactions with the prototype, what do they understand about what has been presented to them? Are there elements of the prototype that the team thought would be useful that are not or that should be obvious but seem confusing? In some cases, users and stakeholders may be encouraged to interact with the prototypes in different settings that emulate real-life situations. Ultimately, all feedback can be used to create future prototypes until the team feels that they have developed something refined and worth investing in developing further.

Implementation

Perhaps the most delightful point in the design thinking process is when the team's hard work together culminates in the implementation of their refined idea. By this point there has been a lot of time and resources invested into the design process and an idea can be rolled out. In some cases, the launch might look like a pilot or time-limited test with parameters set to test what happens in implementation and whether the solution developed is actually as desirable, feasible, and viable as the team expects. Regardless of the implementation strategy, it is important that the team create a plan to assess the success of the project. The assessment plan should be created in consideration of the initial goals of the project and will also bring in the new knowledge gained about users in the insights phase of design thinking. The goal of implementation is really to determine, in real time, whether the solution meets the goals and fulfills the needs for which it was designed.

The needs of the target audience change over time, and a final implementation may only be temporary until circumstances change. The world is changing at a rapid rate and exploring changing needs must be prioritized as practitioners and decision makers struggle to keep pace with solutions. Continuous evaluation of student needs through design thinking and other methods can foster agility among institutions of higher education so that they are adaptive to these changing needs. The 2020 pandemic represented a significant disruption to the fabric of higher education and shattered the idea that these institutions can remain stoic and unchanging. The need for a commitment to innovation and advancing knowledge in higher education is paramount and design thinking is a process that provides a practical way to bring these commitments to life.

Returning to the example of the Innovation Hub's work with students who were also parents, the idea to generate a conference focused on how institutions and government could better support student parents was carried forward into the prototyping phase. There were many partners who were keen to work with the Innovation Hub to prototype this concept, including the Family Care Office on campus, the School of Graduate Studies, the University of Toronto Libraries, Student Family Housing office, and others. In this case, the prototype was a concept that was described at a very high level.

The team of students took their concept and shared it with staff and faculty who had a particular role in supporting students who are also parents, or a research interest in the topic, and also shared the concept with student parents themselves. Over the course of several months, the idea was refined based on these conversations into a plan for a pilot event which was to take place in June 2020. Unfortunately, the pandemic pre-empted the conference, and the team was forced to pivot. The group came together to reframe their problem yet again and a new idea was generated based on the input of stakeholders during the conference planning process.

The team decided to offer virtual support and resources to student parents and their supporters until such time as a conference could be held. This led to the launch of a website called Redefining Traditional: Making Higher Education Family-Friendly (uoft.me/redefiningtraditional) that offers virtual resources for student parents, an online event calendar, a blog with information relevant to student parents, and an annotated bibliography of research about the needs of student parents. The community also has a Facebook group designed to connect student parents globally in a safe space to share their experiences. While the prototype of the conference was not able to move forward for feasibility reasons during the pandemic, the virtual community was an iteration that was made possible by the feedback obtained during the prototyping and testing phase.

Conclusion

Design thinking is an iterative process that seeks out unmet, sometimes invisible needs and continues over time to ensure that solutions generated are desirable to the end user to meet their needs. While this seems to be a common sense and simple idea, the structure within the process fosters innovations that are human-centered and different from more traditional program design processes within student affairs. The high-level overview of the traditional design thinking process and supporting examples included in this chapter provide a shared language and point of reference for the content within the next chapters.

4

EQUITY AND DESIGN THINKING

M y (Lesley) first days as a new professional in student affairs are a bit of blur. As a white, cisgender, settler woman I was privileged to find employment quickly after graduating, and those first roles were challenging and busy. But one memory still stands out to me.

I had scratched the surface of social justice and inclusion in undergraduate student leader training and built on that foundation during graduate school while studying in a college student personnel program. I had been taught to use inclusive language and, although it felt unnatural at first, by the time I began working I was seamlessly speaking with all the "right" terms. In a conversation with a peer who I had just met I used the word "partner" to refer to my significant other and this peer picked up on the word and asked if I was gay. I remember making some assumptions and responding back with some amount of condescension, "Does that matter to you?"

For a moment, the other person was at a bit of a loss and shared that this was an uncommon word to use in this community and people would assume I was gay. I repeated that this shouldn't really matter, but also divulged that while I did not identify as LGBT, I used "partner" to avoid forcing others to have to out themselves in conversations with me by using gender-specific terms. I told myself that I was gently educating and helping, but looking back now there was also some amount of virtue signaling in my conversation. I was proud of myself for knowing better and being able to act as the educator in this situation.

Later that year, as I built a closer relationship with this peer, they came out. I was humbled by their trust in sharing their identity with me and our close group of colleagues, and then I recalled this early conversation. The context of their identity shifted the meanings of the interaction and after some uncomfortable reflection I realized that I had failed to really listen with open ears. I had failed to empathize because my excitement in being able to use my knowledge and experience to do good work got in my way.

I have encountered equity and inclusion as shared values in student affairs since I began to understand this field of work as an undergraduate, but there is a disconnect between valuing equity and being an active participant in building equitable communities. For a long time, I was a bit afraid to do this work. I was worried about making mistakes that could hurt people, and worried about the embarrassment of getting things wrong, and these worries prevented my growth and true impact for some time. I was too caught up in protecting my privilege to take on the risk of dismantling the systems that benefited me, and yet still proud of my belief in the importance of equity. As a field, student affairs needs to challenge itself to understand that equity cannot be a core value if there is not a subsequent commitment to taking action in the pursuit of equity, despite what is in our job descriptions. It is not enough to look like we support equity—each of us has to do the hard work.

Design thinking as an ethos is built on empathy, but that alone is not enough to fix inequities and dismantle oppressive systems. I deeply believe that empathy is a tool capable of breaking down privilege when it is a barrier to action, but only if we consciously pair our empathy with humility and a commitment to learn. We do not know what is best for others. As leaders, it behooves us to do the work needed to build our empathy and make decisions that impact others with humility. In this chapter, we will discuss how design thinking can be a tool that supports equity, as long as designers use their own knowledge and experience with humility.

Why Focus on Equity in Student Affairs and Higher Education?

Over the course of this chapter, issues of equity will be discussed and one of the terms that has been used to describe people who are impacted by dominant systems of oppression is equity-seeking. The decision to use this term rather than words like oppressed or marginalized centered on the desire to describe this group with a term that indicated agency rather than defining them by the systems that cause them harm.

The true value of higher education has been a significant topic of conversation within the field for many years with administrators and politicians striving to answer questions about why we should invest in this type of education. Improved employment outcomes and lifetime earning capacity are examples of individual benefits to those who receive a post-secondary qualification. At a systemic level, a more educated population has correlated positive health outcomes, increased social engagement and volunteerism, lower need of social supports, and a more productive economy (Cooper, 2010). Therefore, a well-educated society is a more vibrant society. Yet, which segments of society have access to higher education? This question highlights the need for a focus on equity and access conversations in higher education. The conversations about supporting access to higher education have increased focus on barriers that prevent equity-seeking segments of the population from completing degrees and diplomas (McCowan, 2016).

Representation across graduates within some academic disciplines is problematic with White students twice as likely as Black students to graduate with a degree in engineering (Libassi, 2018). A significant amount of evidence demonstrating that race, gender, and ethnicity greatly influence what and where students study is also problematic because it demonstrates limitations that remain present in spaces that lack diversity. Indeed, once equity-seeking students enroll, their troubles are not over. Multiple systemic barriers present within higher education can prevent equity-seeking students from attaining positive educational outcomes. These troubling patterns then persist into life beyond the academy, with many implications preventing long-term success, including barriers to achieving upward mobility in their careers (Espinosa et al. 2019).

Student affairs professionals do important work to advocate and build safer spaces for communities facing systemic oppression and have an opportunity to be collective changemakers.

The field of student affairs has struggled with appropriate representation, particularly at decision-making levels, due to many of the same systemic structures that block access to education and act as barriers to persistence. Professional associations and graduate preparation programs have played an important role in educating professionals-at-large about recognizing privilege and power within student affairs and academia so that they may address inequities through policies, programs, and services. A good example of this is the ACPA—College Personnel Educators International's Strategic Imperative on Racial Justice and Decolonization (2019) which redefined the core work of student affairs professionals to include active equity, diversity, and inclusion practice—something that had previously been important to certain functional areas in student affairs, but not necessarily part of the work of all professionals. Creating foundational documents such as this and hosting space at professional development activities to draw attention to existing practices and structures that reinforce inequity is shifting the culture of this field in positive directions, though there is far more work to be done.

Too often, student affairs professionals achieve a basic understanding of principles of equity and then fail to continue their growth on this competency. According to Pope et al. (2019), "Having individual outcomes address an aspect or two of a multicultural or social justice issue is not the same as infusing multicultural or social justice content into the essential competencies of the profession" (p. 31). Student affairs professionals must follow through with action in their work and lives to live out their commitment to equity and access in practical ways. For example, to read and discuss the discourse on social justice for education is a powerful start, but student affairs professionals must take action to live out these principles in their daily work to create change.

Many professionals working in student affairs can articulate the importance of equity in their work, though far fewer could identify how they are personally contributing to dismantling colonial systems in their day-to-day activities. Actions speak louder than words. More work is needed to help a critical mass of professionals understand how they can carry out this work, and indeed, how they are responsible for this even in nonequity-specific roles.

Often, student affairs professionals who identify as being members of an equity-seeking group are asked to take on work that is related to access in higher education, and education around these topics. Henry et al. (2017) showed that a disproportionate load of equity work that has been placed on professionals who embody equity-seeking identities. Those who are in more privileged social positions are often ignorant of the omnipresent emotional and mental cost that exists for professionals who embody less privilege in existing social structures.

Examples of pervasive microaggressions and overt identity-based discrimination are often minimized as more privileged members of the community fail to see connections and patterns that do not play out in their own lived experiences. Examples that may be dismissed when assessed individually (e.g., being interrupted in meetings, being expected to represent equity-seeking identities without altering work accountabilities, and assumptions about competency or background) create a cumulative load that affects the achievement of positive professional outcomes. The acknowledgment that systemic oppression and colonization is real will not—on its own—disrupt these systems. Enacting real change will require that the community comes together to structurally and procedurally address the biases that reinforce these systems.

Design thinking approaches, with their focus on stakeholder needs (as opposed to systemic norms), collaborative solutions building, and structured empathy activities can offer a concrete tool to disrupt harmful systems of power and oppression. Design thinking as a process is not a magic solution to equity problems, though it can be a powerful tool to approach the development of solutions that can address inequity. Design thinking is a process that focuses on innovations that are designed to solve a problem, and it uses empathy to gather insights into what the key problems are. In human-centered design, designers adopt a mindset that focuses on the user experience and building empathy for the users (Staton et al., 2016). Both approaches emphasize emotional connection between the designer and the users. It is this emotional connection that, if intentionally paired with critical equity lenses and competency, can set the stage for solutions with social justice and equitable outcomes. Design thinking through human-centered design holds the power to move social issues forward by democratizing the process of solutions generation.

> The premise holds that people-focused solutions will garner the most relevance and success. Methodologically, Human Centered Design deliberately holds space for increased empathy in the design process that is attractive for practitioners seeking innovative social impact. In this way, Design Thinking as HCD has been implicitly (and oftentimes explicitly) linked to social progress. (Staton et al., 2016, p. 2)

The core nature of empathy within design thinking models sets the stage for improved approaches to land on equitable solutions, but empathy alone cannot ensure harmful reinforcement of dominant norms. Instead, pairing empathy with humility and developing ways to meaningfully include community members within the process that is used to build solutions is needed.

> While traditional design thinking realizes the importance of "empathizing" with the demographic of focus through a qualitative research phase, it fails to understand that true empathy requires a much deeper dive into *humility*, and, when done correctly, should lead to a transference of power and leadership. (Bingham, 2020, para. 10)

Equitable design thinkers must pair empathy with humility to ensure acute awareness of their own ego and actively deconstruct their own beliefs and biases. Only then can they ensure that there is space and true democratization of the process to honor the refrain of designing *with*, rather than *for*. Doing so intersects with multiple critical theories such as critical race theory, postcolonialism, and feminist criticism, all of which highlight the importance of centering lived experiences and collectively owned knowledge. These critical theories question how structures of power define what knowledge is legitimate and valued (Bernal, 2002). How knowledge is valued is an important consideration when engaging in a design process, which can produce disruptive products or interventions by empowering community members in a participatory process.

Standing in opposition to approaches that center lived experiences are positivist and realist approaches that assert objective ways of knowing and reduce the importance of subjectivity and human emotional complexity as important factors within data and design (Ryan, 2018). There are some elements within the world of human affairs that are by their nature unknowable, and positivism alone is not able to manage the uncertainty that comes from this complexity (Ben-Haim, 2018). Innovation can become a tool to support equity, provided that a critical lens is in place when identifying a need, which will become the source of subsequent invention. Design thinking is an apt tool to disrupt harmful norms since its purpose is to foster innovation, but the process on its own is not a solution to inequity. If the designers driving the process have not developed critical equity lenses, then any solutions they generate, whether through a design thinking process or not, will be unlikely to address insidious prejudice.

Defining terms is a necessary exercise when embarking on a journey to understand what critical views must be applied when living and working within dominant North American social systems that are widely acknowledged to be racist and colonial (Alderman et al., 2019). To understand the meaning of decolonization of higher education, colonialism must be defined and its role within higher education described. "Colonization occurs when an external power forcefully asserts their governing authority over a people— their lives, lands, and resources" (Stein, 2017, para. 4). In the context of higher education, this might include how settler history is prioritized in curriculum, how learning assessments do not recognize Indigenous ways of knowing, and even how Westernized education arranges its classrooms with a hierarchical relationship between professors and students. The preceding examples represent implicit ways that education is colonized, yet much remains invisible to those who benefit from settler dominance, as they do not receive negative feedback from these systems.

ACPA–College Student Educators International developed its Strategic Imperative for Racial Justice and Decolonization (SIRJD) beginning in 2016, after which it went through several stages of review and feedback from the association membership. This document was created to intentionally name racial justice (the dismantling of systems and structures of white supremacy) and decolonization (the dismantling of racist systems through the repatriation of Indigenous peoples and reconciliation for past violence) as the work of all student affairs professionals, regardless of what is written in job descriptions. Taking a values-based approach acknowledges that, although equity work has long been included as a discipline within student affairs, multicultural competence is required for ethical work and professionals must intentionally find ways to progress in their competence as they continue in their careers (Mitchell, 2016). The SIRJD defines *equity*, *diversity*, and *inclusion* work as a core function for all working in the field—marking a change in how student affairs work has been defined and making its title as a "Bold Vision Forward" quite accurate.

In Canada, there are parallel, though different conversations happening that are centered on decolonization as it relates to Indigenous peoples living on land settled and occupied by Canadians. The Canadian Truth and Reconciliation Commission authored a report in 2016 that detailed a comprehensive history of colonial violence that took place during the residential schooling system initiative. This system removed Indigenous children from their families to attend government schools where they were taught to hate and suppress their own culture. Many Indigenous children died at the schools, though records of these events continue to be difficult to locate. The report concluded that this act constituted a form of cultural genocide. Included in the report were 94 calls to action, which included several directed at educators that addressed the need to eliminate educational and employment gaps between Indigenous and non-Indigenous peoples. The calls to action resulted in the creation of widespread Indigenous strategic plans that continue to guide decolonization work within the Canadian postsecondary sector, and a host of programming and initiatives to engage Indigenous students in education and build awareness among non-Indigenous students (Treleaven, 2018). Though this represents progress, there are still significant gaps present in outcomes for Indigenous students and communities.

Design Thinking as a Tool for Decolonization and Equity

Thinking about decolonizing the entire system of North American higher education is overwhelming and can sap the motivation from individual members of the student affairs profession that they can make any meaningful shift. Since decolonizing something seems to be an enormous task, it is difficult to know where to begin. An Indigenous colleague in Ontario, Canada; Ducharme (personal communication, December 10, 2019), teaches that no one can decolonize an entire system on their own, but we can decolonize ourselves. Decolonization requires an individual to become conscious of their biases and open to discovering unconscious biases that were not previously apparent to them. Once these biases are identified and brought to a conscious level, it requires that individuals take responsibility for how they move through the world. In time, with enough people awakening to a new decolonized way of thinking, the system may begin to shift as a new value story takes root.

When discussing decolonization, an understanding of Indigenous pedagogy and how it informs teaching, learning, and knowledge is critical. While there is no single approach to Indigenous pedagogy, as each community is unique, there are some commonalities. These include a basis for pedagogy that is personal and holistic (knowledge is valued, as are other human dimensions such as emotions, spirituality, and physicality); experiential (there is learning by doing); place-based (there is geographic context to place and people); and intergenerational (Elders are valued as knowledge holders, educators, and experts; Antoine et al., 2018). Student affairs professionals can educate themselves and work to develop a common approach to Indigenous pedagogy to apply in their work.

Every human and every researcher holds bias. Upon reflection, it seems odd that it is not common practice for all researchers, regardless of methodological approach, to locate themselves in the context of their research. An important part of Indigenous pedagogy is socially locating oneself in relationship with the content, community, physical space, and knowledge to ensure full transparency and agency for those interpreting the meaning shared (Wilson, 2008). This approach of locating oneself in the context of research aligns well with an equity-centered approach to the design thinking process. Encouraging designers to locate themselves could include an exploration of individual bias in prereflection questions prior to engaging with end users in empathy activities.

The inclusion of extreme users as a common practice in design thinking can also be a tool to support equitable approaches to design. Extreme users embody amplified needs related to the problem being explored, and engaging with them during the design thinking process can often highlight the full cost of inequities that exist related to the identified need. For example, if exploring a problem related to accessing financial aid, the extreme users might be students who are receiving high amounts of aid and those that are not able to receive aid at all. These two examples will be accompanied by personal stories from these students that contextualize and situate the human cost of the problem.

Equity-Focused Models of Design Thinking

Design thinking begins with empathy for the end users, and human empathy can be a powerful tool that can be used to disrupt the implicit biases that can make culture shift so difficult. However, natural human empathy on its own cannot be relied upon to create disruptive change. One of the criticisms of design thinking is that it privileges the designer above the end users in the creation of solutions (Iskander, 2018). If there is disparity between the identity and lived experiences of designers and their end users, there is likelihood that this disparity will become embedded within the solutions that are developed during any design process. The inclusion of end users is meant to disrupt this; however, the activities that occur at each stage happen at the discretion of the designer, so implicit biases can become pervasive in the subsequent solutions if designers are not conscious about how they are building equity-focused disruption into their design process.

Colonial structures in higher education take many forms and serve to maintain power imbalances that elevate the influence of colonists over other groups. The power imbalances play out in how course matter is selected and taught to students, what topics are shared, and even how identity-based data is collected (or in some cases not collected) and used to inform institutional decisions. As these structures continue to be identified in the everyday practices within academic spaces, it is ever more important for practitioners to have structured approaches that force disruption to underlying cultural assumptions. The mindset shift that comes with adopting a design thinking approach can inherently open doors to create correlated shifts in how professionals view equity and their personal role in constructing equitable spaces. Bravery is needed to break down these systems, and this can come from a shift in beliefs and values based on the adoption of a new empathy story. It must be acknowledged, however, that the ability to act bravely in colonized spaces is also laden with privilege. It is incumbent upon those who embody higher levels of privilege to learn through empathy so that their power can be used bravely to open pathways for those with less privilege to bring more representative voices to decision-making spaces.

The following models represent different approaches to how designers might structure disruption to their underlying assumptions and biases as they work toward building innovative solutions to complex problems.

Liberatory Design

The liberatory design model was created through a collaboration between the Stanford d.school and the National Equity Project in 2016. The collaboration resulted in the development of their "liberatory design card deck" which is a tool to guide designers through an equity-focused design thinking process that is disruptive to implicit biases that are held by designers (Cary et al., 2016). The key difference in this process is the addition of design modes titled "notice" and "reflect" to the traditional d.school process, informed by a number of "design mindsets" described by the model (see Figure 4.1). In adding these design modes, the liberatory design model actively builds space for equity reflection into the design thinking process. This is meant to prevent designers from unconsciously applying their biases and assumptions as they attempt to empathize and then create a solution.

Designers are encouraged to notice themselves through the entire process, including how their positionality (with regard to the population that will benefit from the end design) has an impact on their approach to design and what biases may exist in doing the work. The design team is also asked to reflect on how their presence impacts the process and how findings and learnings that take place during the design process impact their thinking. The notice and reflect phases are meant to engage designers in active questioning of their biases throughout their design process.

Figure 4.1. Liberatory design process.

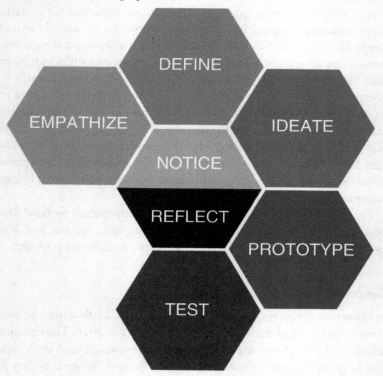

Note: From "An Introduction to Liberatory Design" by D. Pinedo, 2020, Medium. Reprinted with permission.

Liberatory Design Mindsets

Within liberatory design, the concept of a design thinking mindset is expanded based on principles of equity and inclusivity. Liberatory design mindsets build on those originally developed by the Stanford d.school to inform a design thinking process, adding equity-focused evolutions. The shift emphasizes self-awareness and recognition of oppression, embracing complexity, trust and collaboration, and the sharing of power within the design process (Cary et al., 2016). The mindsets lay the groundwork for how designers can redesign themselves as equity-focused innovators and should inform how they move through the phases of the design process using the liberatory design modes.

Liberatory Design Modes

Similar to more traditional design thinking models, there remains criticism of the reliance on the design team's ability to empathize and disrupt their own experiences and identity. There are two design modes named in the liberatory design: notice and reflect. The design modes are meant to provide structure to designers to continuously bring their biases to a conscious level and should be seen not as discrete stages in the process, but rather intentional ways of thinking and being through all stages of a design thinking process (Cary et al., 2016).

Notice is meant to focus the design on self-awareness and situational awareness. It recognizes that in a design thinking process, self-awareness is vital as the designer holds significant power and should intentionally ask questions to address implicit biases. In this way, the designer can bring those implicit biases to a conscious level and act within the process to disrupt them and remain centered in empathy for the end user. Noticing is likened to holding a mirror to the designer and asking them to identify and consider what personal experiences, values, and beliefs they are bringing to the design of solutions. Situational awareness is also important and is likened to a window where the designer is asked to identify external systemic factors that may be influencing the process through the lens of the designer.

The reflect mode then asks the designer to pause and interpret what has been identified from questions answered during the notice mode and adjust the subsequent intentions and direction as this information is processed.

The liberatory design deck shares a series of questions that are meant to guide the notice and reflect modes so that the designer can intentionally identify and process dimensions of identity (who is the designer, what is the relationship between the identity of the designer and end users, and what assumptions about identity are present), power (who has power and authority on the design team, and in relation to the end users), emotion (what emotions does the designer need to be aware of), and context (what is the current design situation and what led there). Bringing attention to these dimensions prior to engaging with end users is intended to bring biases to a conscious level so they can be addressed during the design process and mitigated. The model acknowledges, however, that noticing and reflecting must inform all stages of the design process and there are key questions that should be posed at each stage as noted in Table 4.1 (Pinedo, 2020).

In addition to bringing notice and reflect into a design process, the liberatory design model shifts the traditional ideate phase to become probing or diving deeper into the problem to learn more. When focusing on

TABLE 4.1
Key Questions at Each Stage of a Design Thinking Process

Design Thinking Stage	Key Questions
Empathy	How does my identity and role in this project affect how and what people share with me? How do I maintain awareness of my biases and challenge them to see this community more authentically? What do people in this community identify as their needs? How do systemic oppression and/or privilege affect this community, and how does that relate to this project?
Define	How can we ensure we are reaching a point of view that is authentic and not distorted by biases? What is the larger ecosystem in which our project focus lives? What influences it?
Ideate	How can we ensure we have designed for optimal collaboration and have invited multiple perspectives? How can we create an environment that encourages people to share ideas without fear of judgment and maintains an awareness of biases?
Prototype	What assumptions are we making that we want tested in this prototype? How can we quickly build a representation of our idea that does not require a lot of explanation?
Test	How are we creating the right environment so that it is truly safe to fail? Have we included all the voices and identities necessary into the room to receive feedback?

Note. Adapted from Pinedo, 2020.

complex and sometimes intangible problems, this process can be useful as the replacement of ideation with probing ensures that designers remain focused on the problem as opposed to jumping too quickly to solutions. This pause is of particular value to student affairs professionals who have more experience and/or more senior roles. In the time limited realities of higher education, it can be too easy for professionals with years of experience and education to rely on their own knowledge and "gut" to make decisions rather than taking additional time to fully understand questions and perspectives from students or less experienced professionals. Staying rooted in the problem, rather than becoming invested in solutions, is an appropriate stance for designers throughout the process. When designing through an equity lens, remaining curious in the problem space is even more important. Regardless of the designer's identity, they must reduce the reliance on their embodied knowledge and expertise to ensure that the experiences and perspectives of the end users are centered and valued throughout the process.

Liberatory design presents a helpful set of tools to structure an equity-focused approach to innovation by not only centering users in the design but requiring the designer to develop competency in equity-based mindsets, and to intentionally locate and reflect on their own positionality within the process. Liberatory design offers a practical approach with many easy to implement tools that assist design teams to be intentional about bringing an equity focus into their process.

Equity-Centered Community Design

Similar to liberatory design, another design model that incorporates intentional structures to address equity is equity-centered community design (ECCD). Whereas liberatory design focuses on structuring disruption to the design team's implicit biases, ECCD seeks to also structure community representation within the design team, team language setting, and attention to healing. In this way, ECCD seeks to fully democratize how solutions are generated and built.

The Creative Reaction Lab, mentioned earlier in the book, developed ECCD. The Creative Reaction Lab aimed to empower youth as leaders to redesign systems that currently create and reinforce inequities. The Creative Reaction Lab (2018) identified design as a tool that can be used to dismantle systems that oppress but suggested that it must be carried out with an understanding of broader consequences of innovation as "design is the intention (and unintentional impact) behind an outcome" (p. 4). Simply put, good intentions are not enough to ensure that what is designed will not be harmful to some.

The ECCD process that the Creative Reaction Lab built differs from the traditional design thinking model by inviting the community to become codesigners at the table, encouraging self-reflection and humility, and then bringing truth, history, and healing to the forefront while dismantling acknowledged power constructs before identifying a problem. The process is built on the intersection of design-based problem-solving, equitable outcomes, and community development.

Antoinette Carroll (2020), the founder and CEO of the Creative Reaction Lab, suggested that people's trauma does not leave the room just because people are brainstorming, and as people's lived experiences are integrated into their day-to-day life, history and healing must be brought into any participatory process. Where human emotions and experiences are present, sensitivity for lived experiences and possible upsetting and traumatic experiences must be demonstrated by design teams to avoid doing harm to participants. For example, in a story shared with one of the authors, a student highlighted that they felt most problems dealt with by their institution were only given attention because the issue had been brought forward by students who had been failed. In responding to the issue, the students were then asked to relive trauma, justify it, and propose solutions. Student affairs professionals that decide to employ design thinking approaches should consider how they will create safe spaces and equitable approaches when bringing students into a design process and asking for them to be part of sharing experiences to build solutions. Equity-centered community design offers a structure to facilitate the creation of more equitable and safer spaces for honest conversations.

ECCD in Action

In September 2019, the Creative Reaction Lab coordinated a program to address gun violence in St. Louis by engaging youth in an ECCD process. This took place over 3 days and was called "Young Leaders for Civic Change: Eliminating Gun Violence" (Creative Reaction Lab, 2019). A group of 25 young leaders participated in 3 days of exercises and went through the ECCD process to find solutions. The proposals put forward by the participating youth designers included:

- A week-long program for students in grades eight through 10 to help them visualize future success by interacting with "neighborhood heroes"—members of the community who have achieved success.
- A broad networking program to make connections between racialized youth who have been exposed to gun violence and/or successful people of color. This program includes healing care packages to help navigate trauma.

- Developing a podcast with St. Louis natives familiar with gun violence to inform listeners and incorporating this podcast content into St. Louis history and civics class curriculums.
- Starting a support group for youth impacted by gun violence to engage in healing together.
- A gun exchange program to facilitate the safe disposal of guns by community members.
- A digital media storytelling initiative to motivate change among community members.

Though the program concluded with the articulation of these ideas, participating youth have continued their efforts as "Redesigners for Justice" to follow through on developing these solutions.

Distinguishing ECCD from Traditional Design Thinking

In ECCD, community members are not just beneficiaries or research subjects within the design process but are cocreators of solutions. Like action research, systematic inquiry is carried out within the context of the community; however, action research lays out a clear research methodology while ECCD aligns more closely with design thinking as a framework for equitable innovation (Mojtahedi, 2019). Intentionally embedding equity lenses in addition to a participatory design process differentiates ECCD from action research. Through descriptions of how to invite diverse cocreators, the ECCD model lays out tangible steps that ensure good representation of stakeholders and identities throughout the process. The model includes equity designers and designer allies, with the former being designers that are centering people first in equity, who are working actively to make change that directly impacts them and their community (e.g., a Black woman designing for Black women), and the latter being designers that are also centering people, but are indirectly impacted, and use their power and privilege to create space for equity designers. Both equity designers and designer allies are needed to reach desired outcomes, but it is important to center the right designers in the work and decision-making that directly impacts them.

The model pairs humility with empathy as a personal emotional foundation for designers to follow in the phases that follow. This is an important addition that speaks to balancing the lived experiences of the designer with those of the end users and emphasizing the importance of acknowledging and mitigating the influence of those experiences, emotions, and ego to create space for user-centered design.

The next phase of the model is exploration of history and healing, and then acknowledgment and dismantling power structures before defining the problem. History and healing speak to the unlearning that must take place to correct the erasure of important truths and history, how to reconcile that new knowledge, and then work to actively disrupt the social norms and power structures that could threaten to undermine an equitable creative process with community members. In this way, ECCD wholly embraces the concept of designing with, rather than for, the end users. For contrast, this is the opposite of what sometimes takes place during student affairs service learning where students might visit a community to build something, only to leave immediately afterward, occasionally without consultation on maintaining the creation itself or the relationships that were begun.

Empathy and Equity

Both the liberatory design model and the equity centered community design model include significant additions to the design thinking process that shape how empathy is engendered. Disrupting pervasive power structures that change how designers can be self-aware and constantly checking biases to continually center end users are features of these models. The field of student affairs in the United States and Canada refers to emotional intelligence and empathy as a competency within the profession (Fernandez et. al., 2016; see also ACPA/NASPA, 2015), and the approaches to structured empathy outlined in these equity-focused design thinking models support development of these skills.

Another example of how equity can be reflected in a design thinking empathy exercise is the *Empathy Techniques for Pursuing Educational Equity*, a workbook crafted by Stanford d.school and the Carnegie Foundation (Fernandez et al., n.d.). The workbook opens with three prompts for equity pauses during the empathy stage. Practitioners are asked to pause and consider the following questions as they are engaging with end users in interviews:

1. How might this person describe you and their relationship with you? (helps the designer assess power dynamics and relationship power structures).
2. Why do you think you might be having difficulty connecting? (helps the designer reflect on identity, biases, and values that are informing their lenses).
3. What might you prototype when you see this person again? (helps the designer create an action plan to actively disrupt their bias).

The workbook provides another lens that can help designers understand the importance of questioning their biases as they attempt to activate empathy for the users they are building solutions with.

Considerations When Using Design Thinking to Support Equity

Design thinking on its own cannot solve equity problems but paired with intention to disrupt inequities and a commitment to developing competency in equity, it can help produce solutions that support equity. Some of the criticisms that will be addressed later in this book include the hierarchy of value placed on the designer's expertise over the lived experience of the end users. If designers do not have competency and intentionality to focus on equitable solutions, the innovations that come from their design processes will likely have a correlated lack of support for equity. Simply adopting a design thinking approach will not, on its own, make significant forward movement on equity issues, because it is still possible for designers to subvert the empathy foundation of the process with their own biases.

When implemented successfully using an equity-centered process, design thinking supports innovation and disruption to colonial mindsets. When paired with critical theories and research, tangible actions that are carried out during the design thinking process, such as choices of who gets to be part of the design team, who is in the room during empathy and prototype phases, and what questions are posed throughout the process are powerful forces for change. Design thinking works well when coupled and carried out using principles of equity and anti-oppression.

The choices made during the empathy stage of any design thinking process will determine the effectiveness of the result. All humans embody some implicit (those that are held unconsciously) and explicit (those that individuals are aware of) biases based on the beliefs that are held because of lived experiences. If these biases are not named and addressed during this stage, they will influence subsequent steps of the process. The goals and outcomes created during the *define* stage will be defined based on this bias, the ideation exercises during the *ideation* stage will be conducted within the boundaries of these biased goals and outcomes, and so on. It is evident that the initial empathy stage must be centered in a foundational knowledge and understanding of critical theories such as Indigenous pedagogy, critical race theory, postcolonialism, and feminist criticism.

Not all practitioners can develop a strong foundation of knowledge of equity and anti-oppressive practices at a moment's notice. However, if there is a consciousness of a lack of knowledge, it immediately becomes easier to mitigate that lack through partnership, collaboration, and questioning. In this way, design thinking can be used as a powerful tool to support equity if there is care and attention devoted to redesigning the designers to be more self-aware and considerate of equity in the development of innovative solutions. Designers hold considerable power, and they must be invested in disrupting their own power to make space for innovations that are socially just. The need to disrupt one's own power is not a new realization and there are excellent resources available that can help practitioners actively disrupt individual biases during the design thinking process, some of which have already been discussed.

Incorporating empathy-based, qualitative ways of knowing are vital to ensure a more equitable, human-centered process of design and innovation. Recognizing that the impact of bias and collecting a narrow range of perspectives during a design thinking process will create inequity in resultant solutions is powerful. Ultimately, there are no shortcuts to solving equity problems with design thinking. It behooves all designers to question their biases and invest in learning about equity theory and best practices in equitable design thinking as they build innovative solutions. The authors encourage readers to continually revisit equity and ask critical questions about the impact of each action within their process.

5

DESIGNING FOR
ORGANIZATIONAL CHANGE

I (Lesley) have worked at six different institutions of higher education in my student affairs career. One was in the United States and the rest were in Canada. I worked at one college (likened to community college if you are in the United States) and five universities. All were public institutions. Three were commuter schools, and two of those were situated in urban settings. As I write this down, I'm realizing how these experiences have shaped how I assess culture in my workplaces, and how I contemplate introducing new programs and ideas.

Reflecting on my early career, I can see that I was constantly focused on reproducing my favorite parts of my undergraduate experience wherever I went. I did not fully understand how influential culture and receptiveness to change are when trying to build new things. There were many failures and lots of walking into invisible walls as I navigated new norms and environments, and a painful process of acknowledging that my favorite experiences as a student could not be universal. I began to look for indicators that could help me understand where barriers existed and what hidden norms I needed to navigate. To help with this I started to engage in a bit of qualitative coding while I was immersed in initial meetings in my early days at a new campus. I would attend meetings and keep a list of words that were repeated, or that seemed to have special meaning. After the meetings, I would do a quick code of these words to label their usage as positive, negative, or neutral. For example, on one campus, I heard the words "bright, shiny, and new" used regularly in either a neutral or negative tone and I started to understand that the culture was feeling innovation fatigue. On another campus I heard the words "change" and "progress" as negative terms and "transition" as a neutral term, which helped me understand that this culture was already in the midst of change management which was being met with some level of discomfort.

In a small way, this exercise and attendance at all of these initial meetings was an immersive empathy experience for me, and one that would be beneficial for leaders who are managing staff to engage in regularly. What I learned in these meetings changed how I spoke and moved about campus, and they became inputs that helped me define success for myself. I spoke differently in meetings, I cataloged new input in different ways, and made different suggestions to leadership than I might have, had I taken longer to understand these realities. If organizational change is needed, we must have a deep understanding of the culture to be able to support the community through the change, because the beliefs, values, and mindsets of people within the culture affect outcomes, especially in the short term.

As I think about how to introduce design thinking to new campus environments, it makes me reflect on organizational culture and readiness for change. How will employees and students receive news of design thinking implementation on their campus? The beauty of the design thinking process is that it can also be a tool to support organizational change, by designing solutions that can support the community through the change process. We can use empathy exercises to listen to and understand staff and generate buy-in by making them active participants in managing change.

Adopting Design Thinking in Student Affairs

Design thinking is a framework to foster innovation and, by its nature, innovation is about responding to change factors with creativity. In an organization, design thinking is inherently connected to organizational change and culture because the process is really about changing people to help them rally around a disruptive idea. Implementing design thinking on a campus may in itself be disruptive and require a change management process. The beauty of using design thinking is that it can also act as a framework to support organizational culture change.

Working in student affairs often requires influencing student culture and implementing change over time to continually meet the changing needs of contemporary students. Even so, design thinking represents a significant paradigm shift in how student affairs professionals create programs. As practitioners reflect on the steps involved in introducing a process like this on their respective campuses, overcoming some key elements of resistance is likely top-of-mind. The ability to successfully carry out a fulsome design thinking approach requires a state of cultural readiness within the team and the broader institutional culture on campus. But how is this readiness created?

Over the course of this chapter, a variety of organizational change models will be discussed to help practitioners understand the different ways that their campuses may receive a shift to design thinking, and how they might play an active role in building readiness for such a shift. Some practitioners may be thinking about the resistance that words like empathy might engender as they think about how they would present this process to their supervisor, and how the process might align with existing institutional systems, values, and norms. The next pages are meant to serve as a resource for practitioners to use as they decode and assess how they might introduce design thinking as a process and ethos in their particular social location, and also how the process might aid in managing culture change within organizations.

First, teams need to develop an understanding of what organizational culture is to understand and affect it in meaningful ways.

Defining Organizational Culture

An organizational culture belongs to the unique group of individuals that makes up an organization and represents a system of pervasive shared stories that are believed by a critical mass of people within the community. The culture may differ between levels of hierarchy in the organization and there are often symbols, specific language, assumptions, and actions that are considered normal and expected from members of the community (Goffee & Jones, 1998). Some of the cultural elements of the organization may be taught to new members, or they may be hidden norms that those new to the community must learn through trial and error.

Denison and Mishra (1995) proposed four traits within organizational cultures that are predictive of success: involvement, adaptability, consistency, and mission. Two of these, involvement and adaptability, related to the organizations' ability to be flexible and responsive and are predictive of growth over time. The other two, consistency and mission, were related to profitability and enabled proactive strategy. They believed these traits combined to predict overall success, but the norms and shared identity within these traits are fluid and dependent on the individual organization.

The context of unique institutional cultures on top of cultural norms present across the field of student affairs are both relevant when considering how to define organizational culture within a student affairs unit. Each institutional culture varies widely in its history and context, and this results in a correlated variety of cultures. If student affairs practitioners move to different institutions, they soon find that what works well in one culture may have wildly different outcomes in another. These differences in impact may be due to differences in cultural language and norms, different organizational structures, or different values and beliefs. Some of these differences are easier to overcome than others, and the lessons learned can be valuable when navigating new institutions or even different subcultures within institutions (i.e., different framing of a new program for students in the humanities versus students in engineering).

Culture Change

Change happens from both internal and external sources and is necessary for growth and success. Yet why is culture change such a slow process? Changing culture requires change at several levels. The stories about the place where the organization sits and the people who occupy that space are openly shared in both public and private spaces. Individuals also tell themselves stories about their own position in relationship to everything around them. The underlying stories form meaning, assumptions, and values that are often not directly articulated, but will shape how change can be facilitated or resisted (Kezar, 2018). For example, it might be difficult to introduce new responsibilities to a team working in student affairs if there is an underlying culture story of overwork. Or using the word review when asking staff to adopt regular assessments may become unexpectedly challenging if the leader does not know that past reviews have resulted in staff layoffs. Introducing new stories to the culture is simple enough, but the context of who is sharing that story and how it addresses and relates to existing culture stories will define how it is adopted and whether it affects positive or negative change.

Much of culture change depends on how deeply the stories within an organization's culture are believed and embodied by the members of the organization. The phenomenon of confirmation bias has an influence on the level of belief and affects how change can happen within an existing culture. Confirmation bias describes the predisposition that each person has toward believing stories that support their existing worldview (Knobloch-Westerwick et al., 2020). When applied to organizational culture, confirmation bias is the extent to which members of the organization tend to use new information to perpetuate the existing beliefs or stories in the culture.

Change can be difficult for people and one might argue that it is easier to maintain current beliefs than to adopt a new belief system. Stanford's school of psychology conducted a study which illustrates this well (Kolbert, 2017). Participants were given information to consider and subsequently told that the information was false halfway through the study. In each case, participants failed to shift their underlying beliefs along with the newly introduced fact that the stories they had been told were false (Kolbert, 2017). It seems that there are things people understand to be rationally true, but these truths do not always interact successfully with what they understand to be emotionally true. The interpretation of truth is especially important to consider when attempting any kind of organizational culture shift.

Decision-making at postsecondary institutions is often delegated to key units and individuals that have great structural autonomy, which makes organizational change and navigation of disruption challenging (Tagg, 2012). The delivery of education and the structures within academia have remained largely consistent for the last 2 centuries in North America, which demonstrates this resistance to change. While this consistency may appear to show the strength of tradition, it reveals vulnerability within the sector to manage external change factors.

Imagine for a moment a new director has arrived at an institution where elements of organizational culture are negatively affecting their department and its ability to carry out their primary mission. Perhaps there are pervasive stories among staff that the organization does not care about its employees, that successes within the culture occur despite the leadership of senior administrators, and that a competitive hierarchy exists between staff and faculty unions. The institution suffers from low morale among employees, resulting in a poor reputation outside the institution and a disengaged student community. If no intervention is taken to disrupt these negative culture stories, it might seem inevitable that over time, enrollment will decline, which will begin a cycle that erodes financial viability and further reinforces the negative norms. It can appear that diverting this disastrous course is impossible; however, an organization at this stage does have one distinct opportunity when it comes to change management. When cultures shift toward negative stories about the organization, there is a subsequent increase in recognition that change is needed. This readiness is vital to the success of any intentional attempt to manage change. Perhaps that director might gather a team of employees to design solutions to organizational and operational problems. That team could conduct empathy exercises to build their understanding of the organization and the problems it faces, and then take steps to define those problems to ideate and iterate solutions. Employees would see evidence of listening and immersion in their day-to-day realities that would inherently generate increased buy-in to solutions proposed by this group.

By its nature, design thinking is a transformative tool, and for organizations that need to shift culture, its structured approach to empathy and the way in which building empathy connects the shared stories within an institutional culture are incredibly useful. Design thinking can shift cultures by bringing to light the stories within the organization and leveraging these stories to create change. Broad implementation of design thinking can be viewed as the goal of a change process that needs readiness to implement, but leaders can also use a design thinking approach to build cultural readiness for change as well. Design thinking is flexible in its implementation and does not begin with a goal or outcome already in mind but waits until sufficient empathy with the end users has been established before truly defining the problem and generating solutions.

Change in an Organizational Context

It can be difficult to understand how change affects organizations. Institutions are complex and there are many considerations that affect how change is perceived and responded to by individuals who make up the organizational culture. The shared stories and values that exist among these individuals serve to inform and contextualize how change efforts will be received and acted upon (Hiatt & Creasey, 2003). Stories from within the organization offer key insights into the culture and clues that support leaders in planning change efforts.

Student affairs assessment professionals are often at the forefront of managing change, as they are on the frontlines of receiving insight into the current realities of practice and cultural norms within their institutions. In this way, managing assessment is often just as much about managing change, with data serving as an indicator, and assessment professionals put into the role of sharing meaning and recommendations based on these indicators. It makes sense that assessment roles often have direct connections to senior leadership to provide both a constant flow of departmental and institutional data as well as advice and recommendations based on that expertise.

Culture has also been on the radar within assessment-focused disciplines for some time. Building a culture of evidence within student affairs has become a best practice goal for assessment professionals since Spurlock and Johnston's 2012 publication that advocated for measurement of culture along a continuum that ranges from a culture of good intentions to a culture of evidence. The publication identified key criteria to measure the achievement of these stages as intentionality, perspective, critical linkages, initiatives and directions, and planning processes and created a rubric to assess progress on this desired change.

Assessment and organizational change have swirled together in the ethos of student affairs, but the profession lacks an understanding of the relationship between them. Closing the loop on a cycle of assessment is notoriously the most often skipped or underdeveloped step, with a failure to integrate new interpretations of data into future planning processes. Change-resistant structures within education as well as the recent decades of continual disruption to these structures through the advancement of technology, constant introduction of new programs and services, and social upheaval are some of the reasons why data fails to lead to tangible change. Assessment data forms the organizational truth that is at the heart of an institution's culture story, and design thinking presents an opportunity to connect truth to story.

Change in Educational Organizations

The need for change in an organization can be likened to the biological theory of evolution in which long-term survival is correlated with the ability to adapt. The world is constantly changing and institutions that understand how to build adaptability into their culture will be best positioned to successfully manage inevitable change.

Openness to change is a requirement for cultures of innovation, creativity, and growth and mirrors what educators already know about how learning occurs. Learning happens at the margins of a students' comfort zone where there is an optimal balance of challenge and support (Evans et al., 2009). In learning environments, change is intentionally managed by an instructor, yet in organizations, there is not always a structured and well-managed approach to change. A lack of change management can result in stagnation and organizational decline due to a subsequent lack of innovation, or in a lack of ability to navigate unexpected change that is the result of external factors. The lack of change management and lack of innovation and the ability to successfully navigate change can prove to be fatal to an organization. Higher education institutions would do well to intentionally deconstruct change resistance for this reason. This author has encountered many examples of "long-term" or "impossible" projects, such as shifting to digital systems versus paper-based, that were surprisingly easy to implement when considered against the strength of the resistance. Leaders need to understand the roots of the resistance within their particular culture to properly address it and prime the institution for necessary and timely change.

The 2020 COVID-19 pandemic has highlighted the importance of agility when it comes to change, requiring a global phase of social distancing that catastrophically disrupted societal structures and rhythms. Postsecondary institutions had persisted with largely unchanged models of teaching for the previous 2 centuries, still holding onto lecture-style, sage on the stage practices, which were extremely difficult to adapt to a sudden shift into online learning environments. It is likely that the speed and success of adaptation to this disruption will correlate with the long-term viability of institutions as online learning continues to become a more accepted and valid way of educating.

In 2018, *Forbes* published an article that predicted a significant failure rate of colleges over the next decade as they struggle to compete for a shrinking market being disrupted by changing demographics and shifts to online learning (Horn, 2018). In it, the author Michael Horn suggested that the ability of some institutions to innovate and change will define their success, and that the resulting failure of colleges that are unable to adapt will likely add growth opportunities to those that manage to navigate through disruption.

Higher education is at the edge of a precipice of disruption that will require adept management of change. Tools that can help navigate and provide solutions to change problems will be increasingly valuable, and design thinking is an excellent one to add to any change management tool kit, as it can form the basis of finding unthought of innovations that will distinguish certain institutions from the pack. It is important to note that design thinking is not a change management model, but rather a tool or an approach that can be used to create solutions that help navigate change. To fully realize success during change, it is important to consider the possible impact that change can have on complex organizations, and the many existing models that describe how change can be managed.

The effects of change are not always positive; however, in some cases the cure can be as damaging as the malady itself. Change can be traumatic when people are not prepared for it. Forcing change onto a culture that is not in a state of readiness can be just as likely to cause failure as individuals may create shared stories of harm that undermine the possibility of adaptation because confidence and trust are critically eroded. Finding an appropriate balance within the challenges presented to the culture and the levels of available support is vital to navigate organizational change, and there are a number of existing models that can be drawn from to help during this process.

It is important to evaluate the nature of the change happening in an organization. Is it intentional or unintentional change? Is it the result of proactive or reactive decision-making? Understanding what factors are causing and influencing the change should be accounted for in the approaches that are adopted to coach the organization through what is happening.

Formally implementing a design thinking approach will likely require an assessment of readiness within the culture for this type of change. For example, some institutional cultures that deeply espouse positivist methodologies and objectivity in decision-making may not react well to a qualitative, empathy-based approach to design and assessment. Groundwork may need to be laid to make a case for integrating these "ways of knowing" into existing practices or as a replacement for existing practices. The following models can shed some light on how change happens in an organization and how individuals navigate change. These models can serve to help leaders understand how to overcome resistance to implementing a design thinking approach, and how using a design thinking process to find change management solutions may even be a tool that helps to create the necessary readiness that is needed.

Change Management Models

There are many frameworks and models that explore how change happens and how change can be influenced in an organization. Managers have long recognized that the level of effectiveness of their organization is never as obvious as it is during periods where it is being asked to shift. Periods of shifting are when latent issues can show themselves and interfere with intended outcomes if those controlling change are unaware of, or fail to see, the importance of existing cultural stories.

Design thinking can be used as an ethos or as a practice. Introducing design thinking in any capacity in an organization requires that work be done to assess the level of readiness that exists for such a change. To do otherwise means leaving the success of this transition up to chance. The early stages of empathy and developing insights will inherently create an awareness of needs and a motivation among designers to develop new ways to create change and solve problems.

Described next are a few well-known change management models to better understand how one can understand and influence readiness for change within their organization.

Change Management at an Organizational Level

Several frameworks and models exist to guide organizational approaches to change. A leader who is hoping to build a strategic and intentional approach to transition could use one or more of these to support the setting of goals, objectives, and process during change management. Next is a selection that describes high-level patterns and helpful strategies that can be employed to maximize success during transition.

Kezar's Change Model
In her 2018 book, Kezar noted a high failure rate of change efforts (70%), investigates why this might be, and proposes a model to improve outcomes. She discussed two types of change: first order, or minor change, and second order, or "deep" change. First-order change refers to a change that incrementally shifts existing systems, while second-order change involves introducing something new and requires a similarly new mindset from employees and leadership. Most organizations work toward first-order changes, which can be internally successful, but do not prepare organizations to be able

to handle significant disruption to the organization. For example, institutions of higher education routinely engage in quality assurance activities to improve on existing programs and teaching (first-order changes), but during the 2020 COVID-19 pandemic, these institutions had to respond to a massive shift to fully online education, and this required a second-order change from faculty and staff to reimagine delivery models for this entirely new reality. Kezar also suggested that change happens in three phases: mobilizing (establishing the need for change), implementing (organizing and carrying out change strategy), and institutionalizing (commitment and codification of the change).

At each of these phases, sensemaking, organizational learning, and leadership are needed at multiple levels of the institution to influence true cultural change. Sensemaking speaks to the need to bring staff within the organization along for the change journey. What actions and collective activities are needed to help individuals understand what is happening and why? Sensemaking activities might include things such as communities of practice, speaker series, and other audience-focused education activities that help individuals within the organization buy in to the necessary changes.

Organizational learning is fundamentally about assessment. What data will be collected to inform and evaluate the change? How will data and assessment be part of mobilizing, implementing, and institutionalizing the changes? Perhaps assigning staff teams to collect and then share results and recommendations with key groups during each phase would be useful at this point. Finally, leadership represents the need for leaders in the bottom, middle, and top of the organization to take action that provides resources, supports sensemaking, influences others, and feeds information into the processes.

Kezar noted when trying to understand how to mobilize for change, there is often a reference to top-down versus bottom-up types of initiation. Top-down change is generally understood to begin with leadership through decision-making, policy development, foundational strategy, and individual influence; while bottom-up change is recognized as grassroots-type organizing of the user audience and may manifest through activism, advocacy, and collective influence.

Convergence between the interests of the top and bottom must be achieved to sustain success, and this can be supported by leadership in the middle. Kezar's model suggests that top and bottom approaches must work together to support the "institutional middle" to best support long-term change (Brinkhurst et al., 2011). This gives rise to a third type of change initiation, known as the "middle out," where social intrapreneurs are key influencers and changemakers within the culture. Kezar's approach works especially well within academic institutions where faculty members can be important social changemakers; while as faculty members they may not identify as institutional leaders, they are positionally protected by academic freedom to use their voice and influence in alignment with the cultural change that is needed. This understanding of the need for convergence of interests links closely with the egalitarian intentions of forming a design team from community members in an equity-centered design thinking process. Kezar's theory also provides structure and strategies that can be paired with design thinking to broaden the impact of empathy activities conducted by the design team to the entire community. Leaders can connect sensemaking and empathy to increase the odds of buy-in from the institution.

The importance of informal leadership in motivating change is vital and Kezar highlighted how collaboration between multiple levels of leadership is necessary for successful change, as opposed to the more common hierarchical approach to change within higher education that includes mandates from positional leaders.

Kezar's model is a recent and relevant model to consider when evaluating how to implement change at a college or university as it is couched in this context, albeit within a primarily American setting.

Lewin's Change Management Model

One of the most influential models of change was developed in the 1940s by Kurt Lewin, who sorted change into three stages: unfreezing, change, and refreezing (Schein, 1996). His model has informed many subsequent approaches and establishes change as a constructive process after a period of deconstruction. Lewin's model mirrors learning theories and suggests change could be better considered as learning (Schein, 1996).

Unfreezing. The unfreezing stage refers to the breaking down of the status quo, and Lewin posited that unfreezing must take place before change is possible to implement. In unfreezing, members of the organization must be made aware of why the existing way of doing things cannot continue, generally through the sharing of information, data, and external change factors. The unfreezing process inherently unbalances the organization and creates discomfort among individuals. Leadership types at this stage are important to consider, as transactional leaders will engage in rewards and punishment, while transformational leaders rely on charisma, intellect, inspiration, and individualized considerations (Hussain et al., 2018).

Change. The change stage marks the period when people who comprise the organization seek new ways of doing things to mitigate the discomfort of the unfreezing process. They must understand how adopting these changes will benefit them and improve the situation.

Refreezing. The final stage of Lewin's change model, is marked by processes and actions that codify the newly adopted change. The creation of foundational documents, organizational charts, and processes cements the change and establishes it as a new norm. There should be recognition and celebration of success in reaching this stage to ensure it is accepted by the organization.

Lewin's model benefits from being paired with design thinking. The design thinking empathy phase can provide inputs to ease the "unfreeze" and soften the deconstruction of the status quo by providing valuable cultural context to leaders. To help the organization build awareness of the need for change, leaders must first have a clear understanding of values, beliefs, and shared stories at all levels.

McKinsey 7-S Model

McKinsey & Company is a management consulting firm that developed the 7-S model in the late 1970s. It was published in the book *In Search for Excellence* by Tom Peters and Robert Waterman, Jr. in 1982. It focuses on seven interconnected factors that define the effectiveness of an organization. These factors include strategy, structure, systems, shared values, style, staff, and skills. The McKinsey model seeks to emphasize the importance of coordination among these factors versus the previous industry standard of focusing only on organizational structure to manage change. It is a good way to look at how to balance the organizational structures and human capital that are present within an organization.

McKinsey sorts these factors into "hard" and "soft" categories. The hard category includes the factors of strategy, structure, and systems, while the soft category includes shared values, style, staff, and skills.

The hard factors represent things that are easily controlled and visible in the organization. While they are of significant importance to the effectiveness of the organization, it is the soft factors that, while more difficult to analyze and influence, form the foundation of sustained competitive advantage (McKinsey & Company, n.d.). The factors are as follows:

Strategy. The purpose and intentional plan that guides the organization. Strategy represents all efforts by management to set a course for the institution.

Structure. The organization of responsibilities and portfolios, or the organizational chart that lays out how work is distributed across the company. The structure is the most easily manipulated factor in the model.

Systems. Procedures and processes that govern how work takes place within the organization, such as how recognition happens, how and what is assessed, and how decisions are made.

Style. The leadership style that exists among managers. This speaks to the characteristics of the top-down culture at the organization.

Staff. The organization's human resources and how they are recruited, managed, recognized, and motivated.

Skills. The core competencies of the organization. Skills are closely related to the staff factor, representing the collective skills of staff that inform what the company is good at.

Shared Values. The foundation of the model as it acknowledges that cultural values and norms define how individuals contextualize change introduced among any of the other factors. The success of the organization during change depends on the culture's perception of how that change is aligned with the organization's shared values.

The McKinsey model is still considered an important tool when assessing organizational culture and managing change and is a valuable framework when considering where the implementation of design thinking may find resistance within a postsecondary institution. Design thinking embraces emotions as part of the process which can be a powerful driver for the "soft" factors that McKinsey lays out. To be successful in pairing this model with design thinking, however, the "hard" factors must be flexible enough to respond to proposed innovations. This would be a good model to use with design thinking if leaders are looking for ways to intentionally shift their strategies, structures, or systems while leveraging their staff strengths to generate buy-in.

Kotter's Change Model

Kotter's change model is a cycle that lays out a pathway for creating cultural readiness for change (Kotter, 1995). The Kotter model is useful when faced with a desired proactive change that is driven by institutional leadership strategy. Kotter's pathway acknowledges the need for a critical mass of members to buy in to the change that is needed and builds structures that capitalize on existing trust and influencers to help drive change forward.

There are eight steps to the Kotter cycle:

1. Create a sense of urgency: Creating a sense of urgency should speak directly to building cultural readiness. The purpose of this step is to help others see the need for the change through the creation of an opportunity statement that also communicates the need for immediate action.

2. Build a guiding coalition: When looking ahead to the enlisting of a volunteer army, it becomes necessary to have an internal group of influencers to guide, coordinate, and communicate with the large group during the change.

3. Form a strategic vision and initiatives: This involves working with leaders to form a picture of what the future will look like, how it is different from the present, and laying out actions that will move the organization toward that reality.

4. Enlist a volunteer army: This step posits that a large-scale change can only happen if large groups of people come together with a sense of urgency and a commitment to move together toward the change that is needed.

5. Enable action by removing barriers: In this step, removing barriers is a key step to ensure that volunteers have the freedom they need to work across silos and implement change.

6. Generate short-term wins: This step is characterized by acknowledging success to the community, as persistence during change is fueled by successes that are recognized and shared.

7. Sustain acceleration: This step suggests that the leaders use the credibility that has been garnered with the early wins to press forward relentlessly with additional change strategies.

8. Institute change: This final step is characterized by continually reinforcing how new behaviors and systems are connected to new successes to construct long-term habits.

This model is useful when considering how to actively shape cultural readiness. If leaders suspect that their organization will be resistant to implementing design thinking, this model provides some very tangible actions that can be put in place to reduce oppositional forces, particularly by creating a sense of urgency, building a guiding coalition, and enlisting the volunteer army. All these things speak to generating the buy-in that will support readiness for innovation. The model focuses on the connections within the community as a source of motivation for change, which is a powerful way to engage an organization in design thinking.

Change Management at an Individual Level

Considering the framework and models to guide an organizational approach to change is only the beginning. The organization is made up of many individuals who will all feel the impacts of change at an individual level, and there is another body of theories and models that speak to how leaders can understand and influence adoption of change among individuals within an organization. Pairing these models with a shift to design thinking can help leaders map emotional reactions throughout the change and provides tangible actions that can support staff at an individual level.

Satir Change Management Model

The Satir change model maps change as it is experienced by individuals within an organizational system, with its stages of change laid out in a plot-like fashion (Smith, 1997). The sequential framing offered by Satir's model is useful when establishing empathy for individual journeys within the system and can help to intentionally design some of these plot points for individuals. The model does not speak as well to proactive organizational changes or changes over which employees have some locus of control, as it focuses almost exclusively on the reactive journey that employees go through after an unexpected change event.

1. Late status quo—this lays out the assumptions and norms present that set the stage for the foreign element to be perceived as foreign.
2. Foreign element—the foreign element is an external occurrence that challenges the assumptions and norms within the late status quo. Examples might include an institutional reorganization, a funding cut, a shift in operations, and so forth.
3. Chaos—in the aftermath of the introduction of the foreign element, chaos reigns. Previously relied on coping strategies and behaviors may prove ineffective while navigating a new landscape. Emotional reactivity is common during this stage.
4. Unpredictability—this marker may result in anxiety and a sense of urgency; however, this stage can also be a highly innovative and creative time for individuals.
5. Transforming idea—the idea generation that happens during the previous phase of chaos will lead to one transforming idea that allows for the individual to make sense of and cope with the foreign element and subsequent change. The transforming idea allows individuals to identify a path leading out of the chaos.
6. Practice and integration—the practice and integration stage is defined by a trial and error-type learning as the transforming idea is tested. Progress is rarely linear and is marked by the perception of steps forward and back, but with an overall feeling of progression.
7. New status quo—the new status quo is reached as the individual perceives mastery over the new skills and progress made during the practice and integration stage. This stabilization begins to generate a new set of assumptions and norms that will eventually become another late status quo after its novelty fades.

The Satir model is useful to integrate with design thinking because it highlights how the innovative solution borne from a design process can actually play an active role in change management. Satir lays out how a transforming idea can be a catalyst that moves the organization forward, and a design thinking process that is initiated during a period of perceived chaos can be a transformative way to generate buy-in and return agency to members of the organization.

Bridges's Transition Model

Bridges's (2009) model helps organizational leaders understand and explain the individual emotional journeys of employees during a period of change. While it is similar to Satir where it explores how individuals experience change, it represents the internal emotional journey of employees rather than mapping the events over time that influence employee emotions. It establishes the phases that an employee moves through toward a successful transition to a new organizational state. Bridges's model is especially helpful when leaders are managing change that is reactive to external pressures which may need to happen quickly without the opportunity to generate significant buy-in prior to implementation.

1. Ends—the employee begins by acknowledging that their current state is ending. The transition begins once the individual has recognized that change is occurring. In the ends stage, individuals may feel grief and anxiety as they let go of understood norms and established identity. Leaders should focus on clear, transparent communication, offer training support to meet new challenges, and focus on positive outcomes.
2. Neutral zone—the adoption of new norms and the restructuring of individual identity to align with the changed organizational reality characterize the neutral zone. Although not as difficult to navigate as the ends phase of the transition, this phase evokes challenges as individuals must adopt new processes, learn new skills, and manage ongoing insecurities and anxiety. Leaders should still focus on clear communication, training, and positive outcomes, but must also create pathways to receive feedback that can be quickly responded to.
3. New beginning—the final phase in the Bridges's transitional model, new beginning, represents the individuals' acceptance of the change as they begin to make meaning of the new norms. The success of the transition and how well the individuals feel they were managed will define the new shared organizational norms. Leaders must now demonstrate the positive

outcomes that had been promised, show consistency in behaviors and communication, and work together with employees to develop a shared sense of meaning and purpose.

Bridges's model provides a framework to map the individual emotional journey of members of the organization. The empathize phase of design thinking pairs particularly well with this model as it can give language to designers and community members to name and subsequently process their emotional reactions to proposed changes. This model also provides actions for leaders that can support and address challenging emotional responses within the organization, while generating all important buy-in when moving into the ideate phase to generate possible solutions.

Nudge Theory

The publication of *Nudge* (Thaler & Sunstein, 2008) was met with both accolades and resistance to its approach to change based on harnessing human behavioral insights. The book posits that individuals seldom behave in ways that are predictable using economic models, and that understanding human behaviors and how to motivate them in positive ways is key to influencing desired change.

The nudge theory distinguishes nudges from enforcements. Nudges are positive, low-cost solutions that change behaviors at an individual level. Enforcements are efforts to control and punish undesirable behaviors. Nudges are meant to incentivize good behaviors by offering choices and removing barriers to the desired choices. In this way, the locus of control remains with the individual and reduces possible resistance to change. For example, rearranging health food options to be seen first in a store would be considered a nudge toward healthier eating, while banning junk foods would be an enforced behavior that is likely to meet resistance.

Nudge theory is helpful to employ in tandem with a structured organizational change model as it can reduce resistance and backlash to change measures. When considered within a design thinking approach, designers would benefit from an understanding of nudges as it could present innovative change solutions that speak directly to the insights about user behaviors gained within the define stage of the process.

ADKAR

The ADKAR model of change management was developed by Jeff Hiatt in 2003 and focuses on the characteristics of successful change at the individual level, as Hiatt identifies that most failed organizational change fails at this level. Failure can often be linked to employees who do not understand the need for change or the change itself, employees that do not have the necessary knowledge or skills to carry out the change over time, and leadership that fails to overcome resistance effectively (Hiatt, 2006).

The model outlines five building blocks that must occur in a linear fashion for change to progress:

- *awareness* of the need for change
- *desire* to support the change
- *knowledge* of how to change
- *ability* to demonstrate skills and behaviors
- *reinforcement* to make the change stick

The ADKAR model is helpful when proactively managing change but is especially valuable when evaluating how and why an organizational change effort may have failed. The ADKAR model connects to design thinking principles as it focuses on the experiences of those who will be primarily expected to change and guides leaders to structure and design their change management efforts with these end users in mind.

Design thinking could be paired with ADKAR, particularly in scenarios where there is a stable status quo and/or a resistance to change. This model lays out tangible steps to support individuals within the organization to understand the need for change and the steps leaders can take to help them cope.

Using These Models With Design Thinking

Change models represent an important foundation of knowledge that speaks to how change happens within an organizational and the individual context. An organizational shift to a design thinking approach requires a state of cultural readiness to be successful. In many organizations, this represents a second order change, or a change that requires a new way of thinking. Leaders must have a deep understanding of their organization and of how change affects complex organizational systems before making quick decisions to make such a shift, which is where these models are extremely helpful. The models can help leaders explore various dimensions of change impacts by guiding reflection on organizational structures, leadership styles, communications, influential individuals, and emotional responses.

Change requires empathy for the people within existing systems that are expected to carry out new actions within new systems. All the models listed appreciate that individual emotional impacts carry a significant amount of weight when evaluating the cost of change. Culture is fundamentally about emotions, empathy, and stories. We can recognize that bringing in an ethic of user-centered design may be the change that is being explored for implementation, but by its nature, design thinking can also be a tool used by leaders to build solutions that seed cultural readiness for change. Centering people and empathy in design thinking speaks into the need for buy-in and validation that is present in many of the change management models discussed. As a user-centered process for innovation, design thinking is a powerful tool; as an ethos, it naturally considers the need for humane organizational approaches to change.

Storytelling and Change Management

Change can be difficult for people, and because organizations are made of groups of people, the level of challenge in implementing intentional change grows with the complexity of the organization. These challenges and the issue of complexity is why there are so many theories to address these challenges and provide tools and guidance to navigate them successfully. While these theories can help managers support teams and inform how decision makers structure approaches to change, few of them address the role that stories and culture can play in not only understanding change, but also in intentionally designing it.

To plant seeds for desired change leaders must develop an understanding of the culture that currently exists among members of the institution. Understanding individual values of staff, faculty, and students should influence how decisions are made to engage in a process to evolve the culture and the organization's practices. An assessment of current culture stories will help decision makers understand what new stories might influence change in the desired direction. Storytelling and change management are inextricably linked because change is essentially about the evolution of culture and culture is built on collective stories. Changing these stories takes time. Confirmation bias, the reality that individuals are more likely to assess and integrate new information and knowledge in ways that align with preexisting beliefs, prevents easy adoption of beliefs and stories that disrupt integrated norms. It takes nothing less than transformative journeying for each individual to be able to discard a long-held culture story.

As new stories and accompanying beliefs are adopted, they must reach critical mass to manifest evidence of the change. Shifts in individual internalized beliefs are often invisible until they find relational purchase with others who believe the same new story. There may be a lag in the actual progression of change and the tangible evidence that can be observed to demonstrate that it has happened. So, it will be difficult to know exactly when cultural readiness for change exists without conducting an analysis of cultural climate and social norms at regular intervals.

Change Readiness and Implementing a Design Thinking Approach

Organizational change is a complex, multifaceted process with variables at different levels of an institution. This process is much more likely to yield positive and desired results if there is readiness at the organizational level for the proposed change. While many change readiness assessment tools are designed to test individual-level receptiveness to change, it is important to distinguish this from organizational change readiness and to pay adequate attention to both while managing transition. Organizational readiness also speaks to structural and organizational preparedness for change. In Weiner's 2009 article, they proposed a theory that established a necessary relationship between structural (organizational) and psychological (individual) readiness and posited that these two must work together to establish readiness, with the existing culture acting as a contextual factor. Reviewing the previous theories and models and considering how they might work together to foster change at the structural and individual level is useful as cultural readiness is not a static construct, but a shared psychological state within the organization, and is dynamic over time.

Design thinking is a disruptive process that recenters decisions and evolution on the needs of users, rather than decision makers. Organizations that take a top-down approach to change management may struggle to adopt design thinking. However, building readiness for change can itself be carried out through a design thinking process, and the members of the institution or team can be considered end users of a change management design process. This would mean conducting a process to implement change using steps such as the following:

1. Empathize stage: Conduct observation of the community, collect stories, and conduct needs assessments.
2. Define stage: Engage in authentic relationship building by sharing the empathy results, developing insights, and identifying collective goals and outcomes for the desired change.
3. Ideation stage: Build empowering structures through ideation with decision makers.

4. Prototype stage: Establish the proposed change prototype and engage cultural influencers in feedback.
5. Test stage: Continually monitor the structures and psychological state of the organization throughout implementation.

There are many synergies between the design thinking process and change management. Design thinking also has the benefit of being human-centered, and as a change process can be highly impactful, creating change first in the designers who carry out the process, and then expanding that change throughout the community.

A powerful example of an institution that has employed design thinking methods to create change at local and national levels is Sheridan College in Ontario, Canada. The authors learned about some of the great work that Sheridan has been doing in conversation with President Janet Morrison and Catherine Hale, Sheridan's Director of Creative Campus. In the fall of 2019, Sheridan launched its new strategic plan, *Sheridan 2024: Galvanizing Education for a Complex World*, which was the outcome of a deeply consultative process that brought together over 3,000 community members to determine the institution's path forward (Sheridan College, 2019). With a focus on delivering "groundbreaking, standard-setting higher education that unleashes everyone's full potential and empowers people to flourish in and shape an ever-changing world" (p. 3), the plan positioned the college well to respond to the unprecedented disruption of 2020.

In April 2020, Sheridan quickly mobilized the Galvanizing Education Hub (GEH) Task force, a team of seven leaders from across the college, to respond to the pressing issues brought on by the COVID-19 pandemic. They were asked to consider strategies and models for enrollment recovery and academic innovation through a lens of creativity, innovation, and entrepreneurship. Consistent with the values that informed the development of *Sheridan 2024*, the task force was committed to meaningfully seeking out and integrating community stakeholder perspectives. Ultimately, the task force decided employ human-centered design thinking because they wanted to understand the people they were designing for and find innovation, quick win solutions that were desirable and viable. First, the team conducted a comprehensive literature review of existing data and assessed what was working well in other contexts. They also consulted with key stakeholders. The task force worked in a sprint to identify ways to address the issue in both the short and long term. Immediate solutions included creating new programming that is accessible, responsive, and more flexible, such as (a) graduate certificates and microcredentials where students could start programs quickly, (b) developing virtual mentoring tools to support both faculty and students to succeed, and (c) introducing a fall promise or experience guarantee, allowing new students a prolonged timeline by which they could withdraw without academic penalty. These solutions were the highly desirable, feasible, and viable solutions that were implemented rapidly through the design process. Additionally, Sheridan's design thinking process sparked some other important conversations about the need for a local and national dialogue around education and learning.

During the conversations in the insights phase of Sheridan's design thinking process, students, faculty, staff, and other community partners identified that there are possibilities for change both within their academy and beyond. Within the college, as in all institutions of higher education, there are established systems and structures that create challenges for changemaking. The community was so inspired by the types of conversations evoked during the design thinking process that they saw a need to broaden the conversation both locally and nationally. During the ideation phase, an idea was generated: What if groups of local and national stakeholders could engage in this process too? Through prototyping and testing in dialogue with internal and external stakeholders, the idea for the *Reimagine Learning and Education in our Communities Challenge* was born (Sheridan College, 2019). This contest would engage both local community partners (such as local business organizations, school boards, community groups, and youth advisory councils) and national organizations focused on education and youth issues in a design thinking process to focus around a key question: *How might we collaborate within our communities to reimagine learning and education so that no one is left behind and all youth and adults can realize their full potential?* The question was developed using language that aligns with the United Nations Sustainable Development Goals. Sheridan secured national sponsorship for this initiative from TD Insurance as well as several other supporters.

The *Reimagine Learning and Education in Our Communities Challenge* includes three stages: inspiration, ideation, and iteration. During the inspiration stage, participant teams are asked to share their perspectives, experiences, challenges, and insights about learning and education. Teams can submit their projects to the challenge in a report, video, journey map, or any other creative medium. The submissions from the inspiration stage will be brought together with aggregated themes from Sheridan-facilitated sessions and a review of existing literature and projects addressing the topic. This report will then be shared with all participants in the ideation stage. In the ideation stage, participants will develop solutions to the challenges identified in the inspiration stage. From there, judges will select the top 25 teams to move into the iteration stage, where they will be coached and mentored to flesh out their proposals. At the end of the iteration stage, 10 teams will be selected to participate in the final pitch competition, which is the culmination of the challenge. At the final event in June 2020, the community will have a chance to participate in the evaluation alongside the panel of judges, who will award five prizes of $10,000 each. At the time of writing this book, the teams are in the midst of the ideation stage.

Sheridan's example illustrates the transformational power of the design thinking process. In this case, not only was the campus community inspired to quickly take action to address the issue of enrollment management forced by a global pandemic, but they were so inspired that they launched a national Canadian competition so that others could contribute to this discussion. Change truly happens with design thinking and it starts with the feelings of inspiration that happen for people who are engaged in carrying out the process.

What If We Are Not Ready?

Design thinking is fundamentally built on an ethos of empathy and a high level of investment in establishing empathy with end users during the process. Readiness to implement a design thinking approach requires a value for empathy within the existing culture. Without empathy, it will be difficult to successfully advocate for additional resources and effort to be spent within the early stages of design thinking. Education and student affairs are in luck, however, as these fields typically hold empathy as a core value, which makes design thinking a natural fit for designing programs, services, and systems in these contexts. Evaluate the values embedded in the local culture and find ways to frame the new process and use existing language to describe its benefits so that it can be understood effectively.

Change is a long process, and design thinking can be both a tool to support change as well as an ethos for a changed organizational culture. The life cycle of a student at the institution compared with the length of time staff and faculty are present creates very different expectations for change timelines. Institutions that focus on creating readiness and agility to adapt will likely have more success in their relationships with students as they can respond more positively to concerns and issues as they arise, rather than reply that the desired change is not possible. Ultimately, patience and preparation for a long-term strategy is vital for implementation to be successful.

6

DESIGN THINKING
ASSESSMENT

Application of Design Thinking to
Student Affairs Assessment

As a self-described assessment professional, I (Lesley) had always prided myself on decision-making based on data which guided my intuition. While working as a manager of assessment and storytelling, I found myself faced with an organizational culture challenge on my team. We were tasked with providing creative support and deliverables to staff teams across our division such as print materials, graphics, social media, and web development in the name of sharing the story of our division's work. The problem was that staff felt our team was sometimes inaccessible and detached from their work. When requests came in via our creative brief form, we produced materials based on our understanding of the request paired with our expertise, but over time this model of practice had resulted in a deficit of communication and frustration on both sides of the relationship. With my assessment hat on, I might have attempted to conduct a needs assessment to understand what was going wrong, but we had been sharing design thinking as a model for innovation and this seemed like an ideal time to put it into practice.

We gathered key representatives to a morning-long meeting and asked them to engage in a number of facilitated exercises meant to build the empathy of our team. This included some themed Post-it exercises, discussion groups, and an anonymous autoethnography assignment. Our team heard from their peers about daily challenges in their work, and how they felt when they received a deliverable from us which didn't accomplish what they had hoped. I went through all of the autoethnography stories after the session and coded them by themes. Then I created a persona to embody a de-identified story using those themes and shared it with our team. It was truly an eye-opening experience and offered a wealth of emotional input that not only informed changes needed to our system but generated a stronger sense of relationship between our team and their peers. If I had instead conducted a survey, I have no doubt that there would have been resistance and frustration on our end for proposed changes to our process. Without the empathy inputs the data would have dehumanized the very real experiences of our partners. In the end we were able to engage in an ideation process and developed a new system which embedded more in-person contact in the early stages of more complex requests. It seemed so simple once we arrived at the solution, but looking back, I can see that it was only simple because we had all changed as a result of the process.

Assessment in Student Affairs

Introducing a design thinking model in the context of student affairs represents a fundamental shift in the ethos within higher education. The roots of postsecondary education are couched in the assumption that students are empty vessels waiting to be filled with knowledge transferred from expert instructors. To design *with* rather than *for* students, therefore, will require that practitioners think differently and believe new things about not just the outcome of an intervention, but the process we use to achieve it.

Student affairs practitioners have been designing programs for decades, but typically within cultures that require them to justify their approaches and align with the paternalistic roots of academia. Student affairs has been perceived as the place responsible for parties and problems. This reputation for *something* has been due, in part, to the lack of assessment and evaluation data that could align the work happening with the academic mission of postsecondary institutions. Those who work in the field have long been aware of the transformational impact of good programs, though it has been difficult to quantify and share this belief. And not all programs have been as high performing as they lacked a strategic approach in the absence of any assessment.

Building capacity and a shared language of assessment was hailed as an obvious solution to this. Conducting good, outcomes-focused assessment can provide the justification needed to share the impact of work happening in student affairs in a format that is relatable and understandable by faculty and administrative partners. The rise of assessment followed the evolution of student affairs through an emphasis on student retention, to recognizing the importance of engagement on retention, to engagement as a learning experience (Schuh, 2015). These shifts took place without a significant amount of data to inform them, and practitioners have begun to recognize that operating in a culture of good intentions will put a ceiling on the pace of change and innovation that is possible (Culp & Dungy, 2013). By shifting to a state of positive restlessness within a culture of inquiry, positive impacts can be felt earlier, and the organization can be mobilized to take advantage of opportunities in a timely fashion.

As resources in education have ebbed and flowed over the years, it has become increasingly important to produce data that supports the value of investment in student affairs resources and activities. This accountability is appropriate given that postsecondary institutional missions are academic in nature and the relationship between these missions and the work of student affairs is not always inherently clear. If student affairs cannot clearly identify how its work is aligned with and supporting the academic success of students, then it would not make any strategic sense to continue investing in it. Beyond this need to maintain accountability for spending resources on student affairs, practitioners are in a constant cycle of planning and implementing that requires good data to inform change and allow for intentional approaches to learning outside the classroom that maximizes limited resources. In short, it is a strategic imperative to shift toward a culture of assessment to demonstrate value that continually improves practices and fosters student learning and success. However, as student affairs has evolved toward an evidence-informed practice, it has also incorporated positivist practices that can reinforce a division between administrators and students. Current assessment best practices (see Figure 6.1) often mean designing and making decisions *for* students, rather than *with* them. Truly positive change cannot be independent of the needs of the end users, in this case, students. Design thinking approaches can help right the course of higher education cultures by supporting the acknowledgment of students as partners in assessment, planning, and change management.

The shift to incorporate design thinking mindsets into the daily work of student affairs must include a foundation of empathy and a formalized storytelling methodology into the assessment process and the program design process. These are stages of the process that are missing in a structured way from the language of student affairs planning cycles. While we can look at the define, ideate, prototype, and test stages as modified steps in our existing processes, student affairs professionals have not worked from program development models that require a structured approach to empathy or sharing and listening to stories. It is not to say that empathy has been missing from practice in this field, but rather that the approach taken was to position these as desirable traits in staff as opposed to professional processes

Figure 6.1. Traditional assessment cycle.

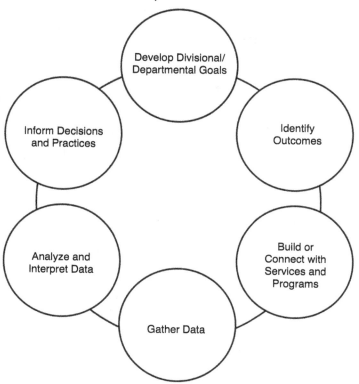

Note: Adapted from D'Souza et al. (2018).

that must be trained for, measured, and practiced regularly. Student affairs assessment professionals have decried the resistance that is often present when working to shift toward a culture of assessment. Staff have feared that this shift would mean all programs must be measured in quantitative ways which runs the risk of erasing the human underpinnings of student affairs work. They are not wrong. The language and structures in assessment circles have reflected mostly positivist ways of thinking and can devalue qualitative ways of knowing. Valuing programs based solely on numerical information does create a hierarchy of data that makes it less likely for decision makers to weigh story-based information alongside numerical trends. Using numerical information exclusively is a problem as it sets the stage for the needs of equity-seeking students to be continually erased from the decision-making process as their data points seldom reach critical mass unless assessors are intentionally looking for them. This presents another point in favor of restructuring toward an empathy-based approach to assessment as it fundamentally supports innovation in ethical ways.

Integrating Design Thinking Into Assessment

Integration of new practices requires organizational readiness to support it, which includes an understanding of the current values and culture (Kezar, 2018, p. 131). A culture that is defined by its commitment to traditional models of assessment that do not recognize qualitative ways of knowing as having equal validity to quantitative methodology will likely struggle to adapt to design thinking. Design thinking represents a significant shift in mindset within the field of student affairs, but interestingly, the assessment cycle that is considered best practice mirrors design thinking in many ways. It is possible to adopt parts of design thinking to create positive impacts without being able to shift entirely to a design thinking process if the institutional culture is not prepared for such a change. In fact, doing so will begin to establish a foundation for the readiness that is needed for a full adoption.

In this model, traditional student affairs assessment models are blended with design thinking through the following steps: empathizing, defining goals and outcomes, ideating, prototyping, and testing.

Translating Design Thinking to Student Affairs

Assessment cycles are meant to ensure that practitioners are regularly connecting their work with institutional priorities and data to maintain accountability and to continually improve programming.

Design thinking is an innovation model used to create user-centered products and relies on consistent input from the audience who will be the primary benefactors of the end product. Design thinking and student affairs assessment are similar in many ways, yet fundamentally different in their starting point. Whereas student affairs assessment forms its goals and outcomes based on past data, best practices, and institutional documents, design thinking seeks to immerse the practitioner in empathy for their end users, while applying their own expertise to evaluate the best, most aligned solutions (see Figure 6.2).

Shifting to a design thinking model is not as simple as distributing information about the model to staff or offering a short course. When considering how to introduce design thinking to a particular institution and department, it is vital to consider how this approach might be received into the existing

Figure 6.2. Design thinking assessment model.

Note: Adapted from D'Souza et al. (2018).

culture. Culture is built upon stories, and the history, language, and symbols matter in the construction and context of organizational culture and its stories (Kezar, 2018). What processes and events currently inform how things are created and assessed? What are the strategies already in place that would work in synergy with this approach, and what structures present barriers to adoption? For example, when considering introducing design thinking as an assessment model, one student affairs assessment professional identified that design thinking assessment would be difficult to sell to their colleagues due to the well-established existing assessment process at their institution. They believed that the name alone would create resistance among staff who bought into a more positivist approach to assessment. Deconstruction of an existing culture can be painful and must include change management support. Assessment is a vital part of change management, and all student affairs professionals would do well to build skills in shepherding positive cultural shifts through relational ways of thinking.

The beauty of a design thinking assessment approach is that it can be adapted to meet the needs of the community. It could be an additional assessment and program design tool as part of a larger assessment suite, as a philosophical ethos to recenter efforts, or pieces of the approach can be used in existing processes to build readiness for an eventual shift to a design thinking assessment environment. The journey usually cannot happen all at once, but small steps, taken often, will continue to push forward progress.

Steps in Design Thinking Assessment

With the acknowledgment that an institution's cultural readiness is vital to successful implementation, the names of stages in traditional design thinking have been modified to speak to current practices and norms within student affairs and higher education. Language matters and while the shifts in terminology are mostly minor, they are important to successful adoption. The most major shift is the addition of the step of storytelling and the visualization of the process as circular. The following pages outline the steps in the design thinking assessment model.

Empathizing

Design thinking begins with empathy. The shift toward empathy is a fundamental transition away from the traditional student affairs assessment cycle that usually begins with setting goals or outcomes. Student affairs commonly cite a high value for empathy (Tull & Medrano, 2008), but practitioners should not assume that their empathy remains active as career progression takes decision makers further away from their end users. In 2015, a senior student affairs administrator at Ryerson University, Heather Lane, began a project known as *In Their Shoes* where she participated in an immersive empathy experience to ensure her decision-making was centered in empathy for the students she served. As she had progressed in her career to her senior role, she acknowledged that she had little direct contact with students outside of large, formal events such as convocation (Deschamps, 2015). To address this, she participated in three immersive experiences. First, as a student in an upper-year fashion design course alongside enrolled students. She designed and completed a full collection of clothing that was evaluated by faculty and spent countless hours with students in sewing labs, sourcing materials, and talking in class. Then, as a member of the Ryerson women's basketball team, she participated in all the practices, physical training, and road trips (though she stopped short of playing in actual games). And finally, she audited a chemistry class and interacted with science students as she made her way through the same lectures, readings, and assignments. Through these experiences a new perspective was brought to her work, as she considered the students she had deep relationships with and how her decisions would have an impact on them. This example highlights that without regular, direct contact with students, it is possible for student affairs leaders to lose depth of relationship with their current end users—students. This loss of relationship can mean that decisions are being made based on past experiences (the students we used to have) or aspirational goals (the students we want to have) rather than current realities (the students we actually have). Design thinking centers empathy as a skill that should be practiced intentionally and regularly to be effective.

Student affairs is no stranger to conducting a needs assessment as an initial step in program design. Building programs solely based on the lived experiences of a single practitioner can be fraught with their own assumptions and biases. Without gathering information to challenge embodied assumptions, practitioners can create interventions that not only do not have the intended impact but can serve to further marginalize students that are already vulnerable. For example, when building an orientation program, it is important to consider that while they may be fun to plan, focusing solely on large, loud gatherings as key social events will prevent students who may be less comfortable or unable to participate in such spaces from engaging in important transition support opportunities. In critically reflecting, we can identify that a variety of program types and offerings are needed to be accessible and equitable in supporting transition.

Needs and climate assessments that investigate trends and patterns are commonly used to gather information that should then be addressed in the program design process. In this way, assessment can be one of the more truly empathetic strategies employed by professionals as it recenters decisions and program implementation on the end user experience, as opposed to the lived experiences of administrators. When building empathy through assessment, however, it is important to balance methodologies. Qualitative ways of knowing are vital to establishing empathy and are valuable tools to build connection and understanding between researchers and communities being assessed. They also provide material that is necessary to build a strong narrative at the end stages of the cycle. The reality, however, is that a reliance on quantitative standards to critique qualitative ways of knowing result in a hierarchy of data, with quantitative data held as more valid (Arminio & Hultgren, 2002). Quantitative ways of knowing seldom evoke deep emotions or relationships within practitioners as they lack context of phenomenon, including emotions (Almeida et al., 2017). Design thinking begins with empathy to activate the emotional safeguards of staff to then prioritize the needs of the audience in each subsequent step of the process.

By shifting the language used to describe the known practice of needs assessment to encompass empathy, it creates space for multiple ways of knowing. There are critical views represented regarding the level of quality and usability present within qualitative ways of knowing, and in practitioner settings, the lack of generalizability may seem to devalue the use of qualitative methods (Arminio & Hultgren, 2002). The lack of generalizability makes sense if the focus of assessment is only on informing interventions with generalizable patterns; however, if evoking empathy becomes another priority, the need for individual and deep stories is similarly incentivized.

Empathy can be explored in student affairs through empathy interviewing, observation, immersive empathy, group interviews or design events, and inspiration. As previously mentioned, this requires a tacit understanding of the biases brought by the designer and/or design team as these will contextualize any insights that are garnered from the process. There is a lot that can be translated from qualitative research practices and Indigenous pedagogy to ensure that empathy is built in ethical ways.

Consider a hypothetical example from student affairs and how it would be a bit different if we used traditional assessment versus a design thinking approach. Imagine a manager responsible for new student orientation trying to develop a better approach to educational content on gender-based violence during orientation week. In a traditional assessment cycle, they would begin by reviewing foundational documents such as strategic plans and departmental goals and then immediately begin identifying the desired outcomes. Examples might be to have participants articulate positive sex behaviors or describe how bystanders can be supportive during incidents of violence. Design thinking would instead begin the process by focusing designers on empathy that could include gathering stories from first-year students, engaging designers as participants in orientation-type events, and observing students during their transition. The difference in the empathy approach is that it connects the designers to the experiences and emotions of students differently, which will fundamentally change the end product. If designers observe that students are overwhelmed and disengaged during large-scale events, and they participate and realize it is difficult to connect and understand complex problems during lecture-style speaker series, they might set different outcomes. Or they might consider designing interventions differently, such as using small group, discussion-based activities or connections within curricular experiences to better achieve their outcomes.

Defining Goals and Outcomes

Mapping assessments to goals is an important component of traditional cycles of assessment in student affairs (Henning & Roberts, 2016). Design thinking aligns with this while student affairs assessment typically pulls these goals through alignment with institutional priorities, past assessment data, and best practices; a design thinking process strives to recenter solutions on the needs of the end users in addition to aligning with strategic priorities. Without centering empathy, traditional student affairs assessment goal setting that is rooted in foundational documents such as strategic plans or institutional missions may or may not be informed by the present needs of students. Relying on data from previous activities and existing foundational documents creates a time lag that might make it less likely for interventions to be appropriately designed for current students. Reviewing literature and existing information is still important to this process, but it should not translate directly into goals and outcomes without consideration and exploration of the needs of current students.

The efforts of student affairs programming should be consistently directed at current students—not the students the institution used to have, or those it wishes to have. Shifting to a design thinking assessment model prioritizes current student input during the empathy stage, and again when evaluating prototypes. In this way, it prevents professionals in the field from engaging with solutions prior to understanding what the current experiences and problems are within the target group of end users. Once insights are gleaned from the data gathered during the empathy stage, it is possible to craft student-centered goals and outcomes that have a higher likelihood of serving current needs.

Design thinking assessment also requires that a point-of-view statement be created to inform subsequent goals and outcomes. Once this has been created, traditional models can be used to build aspirational goals and measurable outcomes to understand whether the intervention has been successful. Establishing this intent is still an important part of the planning process; however, it should not happen without empathy for students.

In the earlier example exploring gender-based violence programming during orientation, the manager would approach goals and outcomes quite differently in a traditional assessment cycle versus a design thinking approach. Traditional assessment would have the manager creating outcomes based on foundational documents and relying on their own knowledge and experience to do so. Design thinking instructs that designers reframe the problem based on insights gathered during the empathy stage and then draw goals and outcomes from their new understanding and empathy for their students.

Ideating

Assessment cycles usually are not explicit about how ideas for interventions are generated, while design thinking presents a very structured approach to what it means to effectively generate innovative and potentially disruptive solutions to meet the needs of the end users.

Ideating will feel familiar to student affairs practitioners who are used to participating in brainstorming sessions and generating ideas to solve problems. However, the strict adherence to an overly rigid assessment model, or the lack of any structure, can trap participants into familiar patterns that insulate the environment from innovative solutions.

At its core, design thinking assessment is about integrating innovation and empathy into existing practices to better serve end users and intentionally shift culture in positive directions. Intentionally shifting culture means working to help practitioners recognize and disrupt norms that might prevent them from engaging with ideas. The practice of encouraging radical solutions to a problem, without editing, can provide freedom to participants who otherwise may frame their contributions to fit within the existing institutional culture and norms. These radical ideas will almost certainly not be the final product but can start a chain reaction toward an otherwise unthought-of solution. To explore specific ideation strategies, please refer to chapter 2.

Recall the example of a manager attempting to redesign an approach to gender-based violence prevention during orientation. In a traditional assessment cycle, there is little direction given to guide how solutions are generated. The manager is left to rely on their experience and knowledge, and perhaps consultation or collaboration to generate ideas. In contrast, a design thinking approach would structure an ideation session with designers to explore the most divergent, radical solutions possible to the defined problem. The end result is that pathways to truly innovative ideas can occur as designers trace these radical ideas to converge on the best solutions.

Prototyping and Testing

Design thinking does not neatly align with each part of the student affairs assessment cycle, and the next two steps have some overlap. Prototyping and testing would most closely align with product, program, service implementation, and parts of the data collection steps within student affairs assessment cycles. Prototyping is analogous to implementation of strategies to achieve the espoused outcomes and testing is analogous to data collection to determine if these strategies were effective at achieving the goals. They overlap in terms of creating a representation of an intervention and then gathering data to understand its efficacy; however, the concept of prototyping is less common within student affairs spaces, where pilot programs are more ubiquitous as a tool to try out a new idea. Pilot programs and prototypes are not the same. In many cases, professionals will conduct pilot programs that are simply a smaller version of a fully realized program. The difference between this piloting and prototyping is that the cost in terms of time and resources of building a pilot program is often not substantially less than the implementation of the full program.

A prototype is a low-cost representation or MVP of the final product, program, or service that can be reviewed and tested by the end users (in this case, students). While Apple would produce a representation of a smartphone or computer for feedback, in student affairs, a prototype for a program could be as simple as a pitch that is presented to a group of students before significant time and planning efforts are invested. The key to a good prototype is to create an MVP that holds enough meaning for reviewers to provide meaningful feedback (Lewrick, 2020). The best prototypes will not only represent the product or service but will allow the reviewing end users to engage with it at some level. In pitching a program to students, it might be possible to have them participate in an example workshop which is followed by a storyboarding activity to help them understand the scope of the intervention.

The most important thing to note within this step is that it reactivates the empathy of the designers by revisiting the audience and reestablishing the relationship to ensure the final design is created with—and not just for—them. The distancing of program creators from the students served reinforces cultural norms that decision makers know best and devalues the experiences of those who will be in receipt of the programs and services that are built. Prototyping is essentially a secondary empathy stage: asking the students, this is what we heard from you, did we get it right? Do you like our solution?

The language of prototyping may be challenging to adopt for practitioners that are used to piloting programs at their institution. A prototype is a low-cost representation of the program to help end users provide feedback, and this would precede the creation of a pilot, which would be a smaller implementation of a final product. Naming this step as prototyping will be important to use as it means engaging practitioners in discussion about how this differs from current practices.

A prototype can be hard to imagine in the context of student affairs. In the earlier orientation example, traditional assessment cycles do not really refer to piloting or early program development, so the manager would likely create the program as best they could with the information available and then design assessments to understand its success and impact. Design thinking, conversely, clearly describes the need to build an MVP that is then returned to members of the community for feedback before final iterations are put into practice. The manager might storyboard the proposed program to educate students on bystander intervention in small groups and then students could speak about the design before it is implemented.

Assessment

Assessment in the design thinking assessment model overlaps several steps within traditional student affairs assessment models. The gathering of data during program implementation, analysis of this data, and interpretation of the results is captured in this phase. However, the mindset shift that is required to adopt a design thinking assessment model will also change how student affairs assessment is conducted as the focus on empathy also carries through to this step.

As already discussed, assessment has been an active discipline within student affairs for several decades, with a rise in interest over the last decade specifically. Conferences and professional development opportunities are rife with assessment-focused sessions. It is trendy to describe oneself as student-centered when working in student affairs; however, if not actively participating in a process to ensure that the actual needs of students are at the heart of decisions and programming, how can one claim that title? It is the job of practitioners to develop programs and services for the students who are currently enrolled, not the ones that used to be, or the ones that are desired. To do this means actively listening and consulting with these students on a regular basis. It is work that is never complete but is central to maintaining true empathy.

There is a hierarchy present between quantitative and qualitative ways of knowing, with numerical quantitative data typically being trusted over qualitative or narrative data. The balance between quantitative and qualitative data is extremely important to consider in this model. While quantitative data can be analyzed to show patterns in data and trends that can be extrapolated to broader populations, it rarely speaks to why those patterns exist. Quantitative data also centers on the "average" or generalizable results, which ignores students and experiences that are not average. In order to explore the question of "why" these trends are present and understanding the experience of all students, assessors and researchers must utilize qualitative ways of knowing. Using both qualitative and quantitative data provides a more holistic picture of a phenomenon. Design thinking assessment must include story-based data to develop empathy and to provide content to fuel the final storytelling step.

The assessment phase is where traditional assessment and design thinking most closely align. Actually, this stage of design thinking almost embodies a mini-assessment cycle and utilizes many of the same techniques to understand and test the functionality of solutions.

Types of Assessment
Several different types of assessment have been employed by student affairs in the past. Each of these types of assessment has a role to play in a design thinking process. Each type has benefits and drawbacks. The following section is meant to serve as an overview of student affairs assessment and how practitioners must shift their mindset in a design thinking process, rather than a detailed tutorial on assessment, as there is a significant amount of literature available detailing how each of these might be used.

Scope assessment. Scope assessment refers to the reach of a program or service. Generally, this equates to attendance and tracking usage numbers in a student affairs context. Another name for this kind of assessment is utilization assessment. Scope assessment is one of the most basic ways to begin to understand patterns and though it should be included in an evaluation process to understand the overall impact story, scope assessment is not a good measure to use in isolation when considering the efficacy of practices in place at an institution. There can be many reasons for attendance or usage that do not speak to the actual success or achievement of the intended impact. Many students might have attended an event, but did they make meaningful progress along the intended goals? Or conversely, the usage numbers for a service might appear low when compared to others but could be serving a specific and urgent need for an important part of the population.

Satisfaction assessment. Satisfaction assessment is used to assess user experience when participating in an intervention or using a product of some kind. In a student affairs context this usually means a feedback survey with questions focused on enjoyment or perceived value.

Satisfaction assessment has been a hallmark of assessment in student affairs and (in many cases) inappropriately used to evaluate programming for students and serve as a proxy for learning (Henning & Roberts, 2016). When used in isolation with scope data, this type of assessment is not well-designed to provide a complete picture of the success of any given intervention due to the self-reported nature of the information and its focus on the happiness of the user, unless the intent is solely satisfaction, such as satisfaction with living in the residence halls, which can affect residence hall retention. Learning is often an uncomfortable process, the seeds of which may not germinate for some time after the experience. While user satisfaction is a valid dimension of programming to explore in evaluation, it should never be equated with learning or the basis for making strategic decisions about deliverables. To do so is to turn student affairs work into a popularity contest and would undermine the foundation of disruption and innovation inherent in a good design thinking process.

Outcomes assessment. An evolving trend in student affairs is the intentional measurement of intended outcomes to understand whether the designed program was successful. Outcomes assessment is a deeper and more meaningful way to evaluate practices as it sheds light on the impact that interventions have on participants. The use of observational assessment, demonstrations of learning, and rubric scoring can provide direct data to measure change pre- and post-experience rather than self-reported survey data. Outcomes assessment lends itself well to design thinking as it is focused on the experiences and embodied change within the end users.

Learning outcomes are an important part of classroom pedagogy. By connecting an observable behavior to the achievement of an intended objective, educators can quantify and measure learning to augment other ways of knowing. The adoption of learning outcomes to measure learning outside the classroom within student affairs contexts is another step on the journey that establishes holistic education of students as the goal of postsecondary institutions. Practitioners are increasingly considering outcomes early in the program design stages by describing what they hope to see demonstrated by students at the completion of the program.

However, not all practitioners are equally satisfied with this new emphasis on learning outcomes. Drawbacks that have been named include: (a) definition: learning outcomes can only evaluate aspects of learning that are able to be succinctly defined; (b) legitimacy: the valuation of some learning over others; (c) fractionation: the breaking up of holistic learning experiences into discrete outcomes; and (d) serendipity: the inability to place value on unexpected learning (Ewell, 2007). Upon reflection, it does seem insufficient to develop intentional outcomes for all students before having met them and built relationships. The intentions and objectives that students have for their own learning should form an integral part of how learning outcomes are designed and assessed. Designing learning for students rather than with them places the work of educators at odds with the need to foster self-authorship for students. It is important to consider this criticism and work to create opportunity and space for unintended learning alongside the intended outcomes embedded within student affairs programming. Otherwise, there is risk that underrepresented or equity-seeking populations might be unintentionally sidelined.

Program outcomes are like learning outcomes in that they are meant to measure observed changes in programs and services that are the result of intentional intervention. Rather than focusing on demonstrated behavior that demonstrates learning, program outcomes focus on observable metrics within the context of the program or service itself. For example, a program outcome might be to increase representation within staffing to reflect campus population or to change program participation targets intentionally. While these do not specifically speak to learning that is taking place, they do support improvement and accountability by naming program intentions and observable measurements that can demonstrate their occurrence.

Needs assessment. Needs assessment simply means evaluating what the target audience needs now and is aligned closely with the empathize stage of the model. Needs assessment has been used in student affairs in the past to understand the needs of students; however, unlike what has been described at length in the empathize stage of design thinking assessment, these tools can be too focused on having students identify their own needs. To be effective, students need to be self-aware enough to correctly name their needs, and they require expertise in the organization and delivery of education to recommend solutions. This represents a situation where the process of assessment can reinforce existing norms if the investigators take the desired solutions provided by students at face value without critically reflecting on the inherent biases that might be present. Reframing needs assessment as an exercise in empathy can help to center students in the data, without requiring self-awareness and solutions generation.

Climate assessment. Assessing climate means taking a snapshot of the current cultural context for a given issue. Tools assessing climate will evaluate perception of norms, actual behaviors, and underlying assumptions and emotions (Henning & Roberts, 2016). For example, many institutions have engaged in surveys to assess their campus's sexual violence climate. The resulting data from these surveys can then be used to inform how prevention and response programming is conducted and how to target different parts of the campus community with communications campaigns. Climate assessment is better placed in the foundational steps of design thinking to inform the design questions and to develop an early understanding of the environment that the end users navigate.

Benchmarking assessment. Practitioners are often confused about the etymology of benchmarking as a name for this type of assessment, which is meant to provide comparisons to measure against. These comparisons might be to oneself over time, a comparison between peers, or a comparison to a validated standard. The term benchmarking comes from the history of masonry, as a stone mark was used to consistently position a leveling rod throughout the building process. The historical background for the term benchmarking speaks to its nature as an important comparative tool for checking performance.

Understanding performance over time is an important way to measure progress and the impact of change. By consistently revisiting past data collected about a program and using that information to contextualize current practices and data, practitioners can maintain an understanding of the journey a certain program or service has been traveling. The definition of success or failure may change depending on an understanding of this journey. To maintain comparability, it is important to carefully consider updates and changes made to assessment tools over time. Editing, adding, and removing aspects of data collection should be applied judiciously with consideration of the impacts these will have on the ability to make accurate comparisons to earlier data sets.

By comparing similar programs and services, there is context built to understand the actual performance of an intervention when viewed against another example. Comparison lends itself well to design thinking assessment, which is aspirational and innovative at its core, and seeks to establish new best practices.

Best practices are only aspirational until they are established as the minimum practice to be considered valid. Standards must also come into play. Professional and guiding associations spend time evaluating trends and approaches to continually update the standards that guide how work should happen in professional settings. While this type of assessment is important to maintaining the professional validity of institutional activities, it might not be a regularly included methodology within design thinking as this process is focused on creative innovation. By incorporating benchmarking tools during the assessment stage, the performance of novel approaches can be understood against existing best practices and past performance.

Resource assessment. Assessing resources is another important type of assessment that should be applied in student affairs practice. There are a variety of resources, including fiscal, human, technological, and intellectual resources, meant to ensure the effective and efficient use of resources by mapping them to strategic priorities. In this way, critical resources and assets can be identified and then evaluated for their potential to contribute to current goals and assessed as to whether there are more effective or efficient ways to apply them to meet those goals (Henning & Roberts, 2016).

Strategic planning. We might not think of strategic planning as a type of assessment; however, it is important to consider how it mirrors the existing assessment cycle as well as a design thinking process. It is fundamentally about mapping departmental and divisional efforts to the broader mission and values and should include early assessments of needs and climate.

Storytelling

Storytelling is a step in design thinking assessment that is not included in traditional assessment models. The storytelling step includes all of the elements of the "closing the loop" step but emphasizes the use of story in sharing data as a way to facilitate change. To understand the importance of this stage it is important to first explore the context of assessment within student affairs.

Closing the Loop

Student affairs professionals have long struggled to continually close the loop when conducting assessment. A traditional cycle starts with setting departmental goals and outcomes, connecting those with programming, implementing and gathering data, analyzing, and interpreting data, and using these interpretations to inform the next set of goals and outcomes. It is commonplace to hear from professionals within the field that though they are often setting goals and following through the cycle to gather data, they are less likely to complete the rest of the steps in the cycle. Student affairs assessment professionals routinely discuss how to avoid hoarding data by failing to use it to generate meaningful impact or change. Too often, volumes of data are collected, only to gather dust in a desk drawer without being meaningfully used. One might ask why this is happening and why practitioners might be failing to truly finish their assessment processes.

Closing the loop is often referred to as completing the assessment cycle in its entirety and includes the process of sharing the interpreted data results, developing recommendations based on the interpretations, and engaging in change management to implement recommended change. The reality of working in student affairs as a practitioner is that time is the most precious resource. Once the academic year begins there is seldom space made for thoughtful reflection. Time to reflect and close the loop becomes a challenge when asking practitioners to participate in ongoing assessment practices that can feel like adding work to an already overflowing desk. Building capacity for analysis, interpretation, and sharing data stories means shifting a fundamental mindset in student affairs. At present, it may seem easier to trust one's own experience, past practices, and continue implementation without fully engaging in a complete assessment cycle. The danger here is that without this completion, the work done in earlier steps of the process will likely not fully inform future iterations.

How Stories Inspire Action

Stories are how humans build empathy. The simple act of listening to a journey through events, especially when paired with visual and auditory inputs that display emotional cues, creates a reaction in the human brain that activates the limbic system, detailed in works that discuss the neuroscience of learning (Bresciani Ludvik, 2016). The limbic system is made up of mirror neurons that fire specifically to replicate emotional responses that mirror inputs. Essentially, the human limbic system is an internal data computer that serves to program behavior. Or, in another way of thinking, it can be likened to a superpower that allows humans to think together and act together simply by sharing stories.

Many might also be familiar with Simon Sinek's (2009) golden circle that highlights how the limbic system motivates behavior, whereas the more recently evolved neocortex is responsible for language and higher order reasoning. This is why campaigns on things like Brexit and climate change, which attempted to motivate behavior through sharing of information, were such spectacular failures, because decision-making is emotional at its core. Rationalizations usually come after there is an emotional truth realized—the nature of confirmation bias—that people are more likely to adopt stories they already believe are true and then rationalize those stories and the behavior that goes along with them.

There is danger in this part of human biology, however. When there is the presence of perceived power, an individual's mirror neurons seem to be anesthetized (Hogeveen et al., 2014). Simply feeling as though one has power over others will deactivate empathy, and over time, can mimic traumatic brain injury as this part of the brain becomes less likely to function. Stories and actively practicing empathy can be an antidote to this as decision makers intentionally place themselves *with* instead of *over* those they mean to serve. This puts science behind the British historian Lord Acton's famous quotation, "Power tends to corrupt; absolute power corrupts absolutely" (Acton Institute, 2020).

The translation of this understanding to higher education requires a correlated understanding of why stories are told by organizations. Telling stories in this context is always about influencing change. As stories are the vehicle to shifting behavior and culture, it means that at the center of every compelling story there is truth, and in an organization that truth must come from good data if there is hope of making intentional positive change. Empathy, assessment, and storytelling form an important shift in student affairs. Empathy is needed to center end users and then assessment provides accurate truth that forms the basis for stories that are used ethically to motivate positive change. Without all three working in harmony, there is risk of reinforcing inequity, perpetuating poor performance, and failing to influence necessary change.

Storytelling is both an art and a pedagogy, and there is a vast amount of research available to guide its ethical use. As already highlighted, names matter, and using the terminology of storytelling will lead directly to the study of Indigenous pedagogy. Storytelling has become somewhat of an industry buzzword in the last few years, though it remains literally the oldest form of teaching (Stanley & Dillingham, 2009). When building inclusion of storytelling into practice in student affairs, it behooves professionals to build relationships and try to learn about Indigenous ways of knowing as previously described. There are important ethical considerations to be made when using storytelling in student affairs practice. Acknowledging how knowledge embodied in stories is constructed and shared with consent is vital.

Elements of Data Storytelling

Before discussing the elements of successful data stories, it is important to consider the audience and context. If the goal of storytelling is to elicit a change in behavior from the audience, then the focus of the storytelling strategy must be centered on what the audience needs to be motivated toward this change. Too often higher education administrators fall into patterns of information dissemination that details what administrators need students to know and are then surprised when students fail to use this information to their own benefit. It is a common refrain to hear academic program support staff complain that students continually ask for information that was delivered to them during orientation. It is incredible not to ask whether the problem is in the system that has been created, rather than labeling all students as inattentive.

Part of the problem is a lack of definition of the desired audience. There is a better chance of attracting more students to a program if there is a well-considered story to motivate behavior in a defined segment of the audience, rather than a general story for "all students" though all may be welcome. For example, a program that is designed to support the development of good study habits and well-being strategies would garner more response if an emotional story was designed to reach students that are struggling with their academics and well-being, as opposed to diluting the narrative to appeal to everyone.

Stories require context. The identity and personal history of the storyteller will shift the meaning of the stories they tell. The need for context has never been more evident than in current affairs where audiences are evaluating popular art and media based on the personal lives of artists. In the context of higher education, this means centering the right person to tell the right story. As always, consent in sharing stories and building platforms for storytellers to tell their own stories is the best way to share. Beyond the storyteller, there is the cultural context, which will also shift the meaning of the story. Recent events, values, and beliefs that are shared in the community must be considered when deciding how to craft stories to have the desired impact.

Brent Dykes in 2016 wrote an article in *Forbes* magazine that succinctly captured the elements of data storytelling in a way that is easily understood and operationalized. He divided up three elements; data, visuals, and narrative, and then explained the impact of using these in relationship to each other.

Data. Data consists of the raw information, written or numerical, that measures variables related to the intervention, program, or service being investigated. The data element of the storytelling process is an important product of any good student affairs assessment cycle bringing truth to the story, preventing the story from spreading inaccurate information and causing potential harm. To successfully integrate the data into a story, a practitioner must have data acumen skill to evaluate the validity of data collected, the methodologies used, and appropriate analysis techniques. Mistakes in handling data or making inappropriate interpretations from available data will destroy any hope of telling a successful story, will damage ongoing trust with the audience, and can cause real harm within a community. The data forms the core of truth within the story and will define the actions that are communicated to the audience.

Visuals. The visuals are the ways that storytellers choose to represent data and/or stories, whether in videos, images, tables, charts, graphs, or infographics. Visual elements take advantage of the human brain's ability to take in multiple complex meanings from single images. The adage "a picture is worth 1,000 words" speaks to this outcome.

To fully optimize the use of visual elements in storytelling, a basic understanding of the principles of graphic design are imperative. Trained graphic designers should have a deep understanding of these principles and how to be intentional in conveying information through visual design using them. While not all practitioners are required to be expert graphic designers to be successful in visualizing data stories, building capacity among staff to have a common language and understanding of goals is needed to be able to evaluate visual design decisions against the desired outcome of the story.

It is also important to distinguish between aesthetic and design in this element. Good graphic design accomplishes a job but may not be something that all people want to hang in their home. Building visuals, especially if working with a trained graphic designer, can be a frustrating and fruitless task if mired in aesthetic versus meaningful changes in the message being conveyed. For example, practitioners might feel strongly about color scheme or positioning of information being applied to a visual representing excerpts from a data set, but if they are working with a designer who understands the principles of design, they would be best advised to give feedback on the design only if the colors or positioning are interfering with the meaning of the information, rather than whether they personally like it.

Narrative. The narrative encompasses all the context, the characters, the setting, and the journey through events. Good stories always have a challenge and clear stakes; why should the audience care about what is happening in the story? What does it mean if the challenge is not met? The narrative might be spoken or written, but is always a human detailing the beginning, middle, and end of events (even if the end is a call to the audience to be part of crafting the desired ending). The narrative is where the emotional impact of the story must be placed, so academic and corporate-style language will not evoke the desired reaction. It takes practice and vulnerability to be authentic enough to create this emotional relatability in a narrative. Academia has glorified objectivity, but when the outcome of the story is to influence change, objectivity becomes a barrier to motivating people. Working toward objectivity is paramount in the gathering of data (though one can never truly eliminate bias), but subjectivity is the storyteller's best friend.

Assessment professionals often craft reports to share data analysis findings, and this is an important opportunity to bring narrative into the dissemination of data. What story-based examples can be brought into the findings to create plot and shape the impact of the data? There could be de-identified narrative used to reference supporting data points ensuring the story accurately reflects the findings. The emotional impact of a human-centered story is ultimately needed to motivate the effective use of the data.

Combining the elements. It is common to see two of these elements combined at a time and each of these combinations accomplishes something specific in the audience. Combining data and narrative explains something and an example would be a good report produced that details data within a human retelling of events. When data is combined with visuals, this will enlighten the audience, and this can be seen in any chart, graph, or basic infographic (a good infographic might combine all three). And finally, joining visuals with narrative will engage the audience. The appeal of visuals is apparent by the billions of dollars spent on the media industry and the trend of "binging" on streamed video content. Visual storytelling literally hijacks the human brain and can be addictive, but this psychology is put to good use if we can make data stories similarly engaging.

Combining all three of these elements together will influence change, though the effectiveness with which the story is crafted will decide if the change is as intended. Once a story is sent out to the audience, it becomes part of the community's story and subject to change and reinterpretation. There is significant skill required to anticipate the needs of the audience and accurately predict their reaction to new information. The strength of the design thinking assessment model is in couching the resulting story in the empathy established during the early stages and subsequently revisited throughout the process, as this will anchor the final story firmly within the culture and make change more predictable. Successful combinations of all three elements might look like a well-planned infographic relating a narrative using data visualizations, a video story containing references to data, or even a well-crafted blog post or report highlighting data with effective visualizations while capturing an illustrative narrative to humanize the impact.

In practice, student affairs professionals often fail to "close the loop" on traditional assessment cycles. Consider again the manager who is tasked with building a new approach to gender-based violence prevention during orientation. They might have conducted assessments on their intervention and possibly included the results in a report, but it is much less likely that there were meaningful changes to the program in subsequent years due to intentional review of the report. By incorporating storytelling into their design thinking model, the manager would have to construct an intentional story for their audiences to influence change in the community. That might include a narrative report to decision makers, couched in data, as well as a social media campaign to further educate students using transformational stories told by their peers who attended the program during orientation. These stories would change the community by degrees resulting in an influenced movement in values and beliefs to set the stage for next year's programming.

Final Considerations

Design thinking assessment is a significant shift in practice for student affairs. Adopting it fully may be challenging until a state of institutional readiness is created. However, the strength of this model is that it may be introduced as an additional assessment tool or as an ethos of practice. Either way, implementation will require the development of staff capacity in basic assessment skills, qualitative ways of knowing, equity, and communications and marketing. It can be applied within program-level design, organizational design, and cultural mindset activities depending on the needs and readiness of the institution.

7

DISCUSSION OF
CHALLENGES AND
LIMITATIONS

The preceding pages have devoted much time and thought to presenting a case for the use of design thinking in student affairs. Time has been devoted to outlining the process with examples and applications to other topics. Yet every framework has limits and not every tool can be used to solve every problem. Perhaps Abraham Maslow put this most eloquently in his book *The Psychology of Science* (1966) where he stated, "If all you have is a hammer, everything looks like a nail" (p. 15). There are many problems that should be addressed with an approach far different than design thinking. Where one wishes to examine wicked problems through a human-centered lens and has the time to commit to the process, design thinking is appropriate. To be clear, design thinking is certainly not a one-size-fits-all problems framework or method.

Why Discuss Challenges and Limitations?

For student affairs practitioners and leaders, design thinking can be but one tool in a larger tool kit of resources and is one of many resources to draw on to create innovation and change. This chapter is presented as a discussion of the critiques and challenges with design thinking. Aiming to provide a comprehensive overview of each criticism, the authors also offer some insight into some collective thoughts about each critique and/or limitation. The authors offer an opportunity for readers to think more deeply through a critical lens about this method and draw their own conclusions about its efficacy.

Overview of Design Thinking Criticism— Challenges and Limitations

Design thinking, while powerful in many ways, is not without its imperfections and is not a one-size-fits-all approach. The critiques of design thinking relate to the limits of its application, the experience of the design team, and its ability to truly generate solutions that lead to transformational innovation. In addition, there are challenges to implementation and limitations to the application of design thinking that are important to consider. Implementing a design thinking approach can be challenging mostly due to the time required to conduct the process, but also because of the time and resources needed to build the lead designer's competency on the approach as well as in the subject area of the solution. Even with all of these considerations taken into account, design thinking represents a significant change and disruption to the existing culture of academia which must be shifted to a state of readiness in order to host an effective design thinking assessment process. Finally, the nature of this model digs deeply into the present experience of end users, which can very often be highly insightful, but does not always effectively predict the needs of the end users of tomorrow and the impact of future possibilities on the present-day realities that users face.

Criticisms of Design Thinking

With any method or approach, there are promoters and detractors, and design thinking has its supporters and critics. Those expressing criticism have suggested several challenges with design thinking and concluded that it is not a silver bullet or magic method. The following pages outline some of the themes of criticism that come up in relation to this method. The internet is filled with essays and opinion pieces about design thinking, as it can be a controversial topic, and there is a wide range of opinions about it. Some critics have even pointed out that design thinking actually lacks criticism, perhaps the most ironic criticism of all, given the healthy amount of criticism the authors have noted in this volume of design thinking. It is important to note that the authors of this book do not believe that design thinking is appropriate in every context or to address every problem or challenge. It is just one inclusive and equitable approach for issues or challenges where the end user's experience can be prioritized, which fills a gap in higher education due to the propensity to limit student involvement in academic design and decision-making spaces.

The critiques of design thinking tend to have some common themes that this chapter will explore in more depth. One is that traditional design thinking processes do not adequately support equity due to a lack of inherent biases that often go unaddressed among designers. This is explored at length in chapter 4. Other criticisms that we will explore here are that design thinking is too prescriptive and can be jargony, emphasizing the overuse of words such as innovation, which leads to their perception as buzzwords. Another theme is that design thinking runs the risk of perpetuating the status quo, particularly in organizations that are conservative when it comes to change, or where strong power dynamics exist. Finally, critics assert that that design thinking is too often portrayed as a magic bullet, one-size-fits-all problems approach without adequate discussion about its limitations. They wonder if the excitement about the process and its relatively quick spread are just hype or if design thinking is a worthwhile endeavor. The remainder of this chapter is a summary of each of these points that examines each criticism through examples of arguments made for each.

Design Thinking Lacks Criticism

The assertion that design thinking lacks criticism appears to be unfounded, given the extensive volume of criticism that is available through research. Award-winning designer and branding expert Natasha Jen gave a talk at the 2018 Design Indaba summit entitled *Design Thinking is B.S.* In this talk, Jen emphasized that in design, criticism (or *crit* as it is referred to in the design community) is incredibly important to legitimize any method. In the design profession, Jen emphasized, criticism is constant. Good designers are self-critical and constantly reflective, seeking to improve or refine their designs, and looking at designs from various perspectives. Jen shared her sentiment that it is rare to come across academic criticism of design thinking as a method, which, based on her argument, is misaligned with the design profession's deep value for critique of the work, including methods and approaches in addition to the designs themselves.

Jen's point about the need for crit is well-taken. Since her talk, the criticism of design thinking has grown and there is a significant amount of commentary about the limitations of design thinking, which will be shared in the following pages. Much of the criticism is presented online in blogs and opinion pieces by practitioners. There is a limited amount of academic research on the topic of design thinking. There is an opportunity for design thinking's effectiveness and long-term impact to be studied and findings published.

Design Thinking Is Too Prescriptive and Uses Too Much Jargon

The perception of design thinking as a formulaic or prescriptive model for something that should be creative and exploratory represents a common criticism. Some have argued that the many models for design thinking are too linear and do not follow a creative process. Returning to Jen's 2018 talk, the designer showed visuals of the various design thinking models and criticized their linear design. She spoke of true design as a creative process that is nonlinear yet showed, in contrast, images of design thinking models that are all depicted as linear processes. She suggested that there is a need to think about design not as prescriptive and linear, but as a true exploration.

Jen went on to share images of Post-it notes, a hallmark of design thinking, and reminded listeners that the content of these Post-it notes are just thoughts from people's heads. She believed that using Post-it notes to capture thoughts can limit creativity and suggested that there are other materials that can be brought into this process. Her belief is that design thinking has tried to democratize design and repackaged ideas (i.e., empathy) which have been commonplace in numerous methods and simplified as listening to customers. Jen's point is well-taken. The core concepts and methods used in design thinking processes are not new.

Empathizing with users is done through qualitative data collection and is certainly not unique to design thinking. The idea of innovation is not new, and the countless examples of innovations and innovative practices throughout history were not all born from a design thinking process. Furthering her point, Jen discussed the jargon often seen in language used in association with design thinking. For example, she cites words like "unleash" and "unlock" that are often heard in design circles and questioned the true meaning of these words. Jen's critique of the jargon found in design thinking circles aligns with her perspective on innovation—that for something to truly be an innovation it must be realized in the world. In other words, there is no innovation unless there is a tangible outcome, a product taken to market, for example. Many design thinking projects may yield valuable information about users, but they do not result in innovation unless a successfully implemented outcome that is truly desirable, feasible, and viable is created.

Similar criticism that design thinking is an overly popular method, rife with jargon and lacking evidence-based approaches, can be found in various articles. For example, psychologist and innovation designer Cameron D. Norman (2017) offered a similar perspective to Jen's about the pitfalls of design thinking. Norman suggested that while design thinking brings a concrete approach that makes design more tangible to those who feel they may lack creativity or do not think of themselves as designers, there is a lack of documentation in the process which supports the idea that design thinking is merely hype that leads to elevated expectations. Norman's points certainly raise valid concerns and call into question the ability of a design thinking process to formulaically create innovations that truly meet human needs and bring useful novelty into the world.

In a later 2017 article, Norman reiterated the challenge that design thinking does not consistently deliver on its promise and questioned the idea that the design thinking models are somehow scientific or foolproof methods to create truly novel solutions that meet user needs. Interestingly, Norman's discussion on the inconsistent results produced by design thinking raises an important question: Is design thinking a creative process or a scientific method or both? Is this another example of qualitative ways of knowing being held to account against positivist standards? Or does the answer to this criticism rest in integrating principles of scientific research into the process? Does design thinking require a label or does the process really fall somewhere between an art and a science? Does it matter if we call it one or the other?

Perhaps design thinking is a mix of best practices from both arts-based approaches as well as scientific research. For example, at the University of Toronto Innovation Hub, leading students to the creative aspects of design thinking requires them to step outside of their academic roles where they are often trained in formal scientific research methods and help them bring in creative thinking using various arts-based practices. Often students are encouraged to draw during data analysis. They might be asked to draw something that represents or conveys the data without words. Other times free-flow creative writing exercises are used to help with processing their thoughts or even dramatize the data in order to build more empathy or better understand the perspectives of different stakeholders. With all this in mind, the student designers still apply best practices from their research including how data is collected, stored, and coded in a qualitative research software platform, and how consent is obtained, for example. In its execution, design thinking can be both science and art.

Returning to the discussion about the criticism of design thinking jargon, this concern is echoed by Lee Vinsel (2018), assistant professor of science, technology, and society at Virginia Tech, in his article in *The Chronicle of Higher Education* entitled "Design Thinking Is a Boondoggle." In this article, Vinsel suggested that design thinkers are infamous for using jargon that sounds scientific with the intention of overinflating the importance of design thinking or suggesting that their technique is special. Vinsel specifically criticized some of the terms used in design thinking, such as the word *reframe*, which describes the process of changing perspective when looking at a problem. Design thinking certainly provides ample amounts of unusual vocabulary to illustrate various functions. Vinsel's perspective on jargon is interesting because one could argue that any field builds a shared terminology that is difficult for the outside world to understand. When are common words considered jargon and at what point do shared language and norms become evidence of a culture?

The world of innovation in business is also filled with its keywords. Higher education, like any professional field, also has its own jargon. Vinsel noted that, although much innovation took place before World War II, the word innovation only increased after 1945, particularly in the 1960s and 1990s. Since then, the explosion of growth of industry in Silicon Valley generated a correlated lexicon which expanded to include other terms such as *thought-leaders*, *change-agents*, *disruption*, and other terminology. Vinsel posited that this innovation vocabulary compensates for an actual scarcity of truly innovative change and technological developments. The use of jargon in the design thinking world certainly generates a great amount of criticism and calls into question the need to use new language to describe old problems. At the core of this criticism is the question of whether jargon is used as a distraction from the pitfalls of the method itself. If so, then it is possible that design thinking is a time-limited hype that will die as quickly as it rose to popularity.

It is important to note to readers that this book certainly contains some of the design thinking jargon mentioned by critics. But, sometimes, use of jargon is required to accurately depict and explain concepts. The solution may not necessarily be to replace jargon, but to define terms and language used.

Design Thinking Is All Hype

Questions about whether design thinking is overly hyped as the "next big thing" in business, or whether there is truly substance behind it, may be due to the model's rapid rise to popularity. In a 2019 article entitled "Exploring the Reasons for Design Thinking Criticism," architect, designer, and UX researcher Shane Ketterman provided a brief history of design thinking. Ketterman suggested that the design thinking approach has emerged slowly over the past 50 years as an approach to problem-solving. He explained that in 1969 a design process was applied to engineering and science and later applied as a more democratic process of architectural design in the 1980s. In 1982, Ketterman shared, design thinking was introduced by Nigel Cross in the United Kingdom as a field of study, and finally applied to business problems in the early 1990s by David M. Kelley at the IDEO consultancy. Reflecting on this history, Ketterman suggested that contemporary design thinking has become superficial and that its rising popularity since the early 1990s could have become a weakness.

Further into his critical analysis of design thinking, Ketterman reminded readers that the business community has a history of quickly adopting frameworks and systems. He cites the Total Quality Management (TQM) system designed to generate continuous improvement in manufacturing as an example of a method that became a victim of its own popularity after a rapid and widespread adoption across the manufacturing sector. Ketterman shared the TQM cautionary tale as a close comparison to the way that design thinking has risen to popularity and warned that widespread ineffective implementation of design thinking across the business community could result in a mass decline in popularity, as quickly as it rose to that status. Ketterman alluded to the business community's propensity to create corporate checkboxes for things like innovation and productivity and warned that the reduction of design thinking to a simple process that can be learned in a short span of time is dangerous and diminishes the expertise that is required to design effectively. Design is only a process, which must be coupled with competencies, and the rapid adoption of design thinking in the business world may be guilty of diminishing the skills and training required to truly design well. If so, some criticism must be assessed as to whether it speaks to the model, or the lack of effort put forward by organizations to build appropriate capacity to design.

Design Thinking Preserves the Status Quo

While design thinking is an approach to innovation that claims to disrupt present circumstances by creating different solutions to old problems, some critics argue that it not only does not accomplish this, but actually runs the risk of being too conservative, and protecting the status quo. In her 2018 *Harvard Business Review* article, Natasha Iskander claimed that most design thinking critics have missed something. Iskander argued that by privileging the designer above all others, the method becomes a strategy that preserves the status quo by turning the ability to solve problems into a practice that is limited to those who follow the prescriptive design thinking methodology. Iskander compared design thinking to a past approach to problem-solving known as the rational-experimental approach that was popularized in the 1970s–1980s where problem-solving would happen over a series of stages similar to those outlined in design. She went on to emphasize that the key difference between rational-experimental problem-solving and design thinking is that the former approach relied on existing data about the issue, whereas design thinking endeavors to collect new insights through the empathy approach, but that the models are otherwise comparable.

In the same article, Iskander argued that design thinking protects the perspectives of the most powerful and that the designer, usually in a position of power and influence and motivated to preserve the status quo, is empowered to select the winning idea options generated. While elements of the design thinking process are mentioned in the article, seeking feedback from the populations targeted by the design through prototyping and testing, Iskander argued that the designer is usually the person who often makes the final decisions, therefore preserving the status quo.

Similar criticisms have been declared by others. In a 2019 online article in *Print* magazine, Ellen Shapiro echoed some of the criticism from Natasha Jen's critical talk about design thinking, specifically regarding the actual innovations resulting from the design process. She emphasized that corporate money is often spent on solutions that seem quite obvious and may not have required such a lengthy process, citing examples like using stickers on an MRI machine to make it more palatable for young children or using younger models in ads for antiaging creams. Shapiro discussed rigidity as a problem with design thinking's five questions and whether these steps are producing truly revolutionary products or services that better meet user needs. She wonders if the steps of the design process have the potential to preserve the status quo by generating solutions that are variations of what already exists. Shapiro's article, however, did mention the advantage of the process in generating a deep understanding of user needs to find the nuances that serve as inspiration for new ideas.

There are some important points raised in the criticism that mindlessly following a design thinking process may perpetuate the status quo and protect the powerful. This criticism also raises important questions around who is positioned as the lead designer and what leadership of a design team could or should look like. These questions relate deeply to the need for equity to be a key consideration when approaching design thinking and positions the equity-focused models covered in chapter 3 as potential solutions to these problems. Ultimately, the potential for the design process to inadvertently perpetuate a conservative approach to problem-solving that mirrors similar conservative processes that have proven unsuccessful in the past merits critical thought.

Other Design Thinking Criticism

While the academic criticism of design thinking is sparse, online criticism certainly does exist and raises important points to consider. Some additional criticisms of design thinking that do not form themes as broadly touch on its vagueness in approach, claims that the process is a magic-bullet or one-size-fits-all approach, simply a corporate check box, and that it actually places too much focus on the end user. There is much to be learned from each critic's perspective as organizations and institutions seek to make considerations for the way they choose to employ the method in their own context.

The idea that design thinking is too vague in its approach was explored in a 2017 essay by Lee Vinsel, the assistant professor of science, technology, and society at Virginia Tech cited earlier. In this essay written for Medium he argued that design thinking becomes increasingly vague the more deeply it is explored. Vinsel emphasized that design thinking has been inflated as an approach that can solve all problems; yet, when one looks more closely it is vapid and uninspired. Vinsel's impression of those who follow design thinking is that they are cultlike in their adoption and suggested claims that design thinking can solve large systemic issues and political challenges is nonsense.

Recall that Shane Ketterman (2019) cautioned organizations that design thinking can become a corporate check box, creating an organizational mentality which succumbs to the drive to innovate. Then, fully on board the design thinking bandwagon, they neglect the need for adequate time and space needed to fuel the fires of creativity. Similarly, Steve Brown (2019) argued that over 70% of digital innovations born from design thinking fail in part because organizations fail to appreciate the culture shift required for design thinking to be successfully implemented. Cultural readiness for design thinking requires considerations for context and the organization's actual ability to implement and sustain the proposed solution. Ketterman noted the tendency for design thinking to inflate the importance of end user desirability for the solution, without considering other organizational and cultural factors that give meaningful context to the problem. He suggests that all these factors must be considered when ideating solutions.

While academic criticism of design thinking is limited, and the method has not been professionally researched in academic publications, there are many criticisms of the approach. Critical perspectives are always important to explore and can offer useful insights for the considerations that higher education institutions should make when thinking about using this method. In the following section of this chapter, the authors' thoughts in response to these criticisms are offered as a commentary.

Responses to Criticism

To round out the discussion of design thinking criticism, the authors offer the following pages to respond and share potential opposing views. Despite the criticism, many authors have defended design thinking and offered responses to critics. The following section outlines some of these responses to the criticism, and in some cases poses additional questions, or makes suggestions to further practice in higher education contexts.

Arguments that design thinking is too formulaic or prescriptive, that it takes an overly linear approach to a process that should be highly creative, and suggestions that innovation has become over emphasized were presented. These limitations should be interrogated, especially in higher education and student affairs contexts where academic research is held as the standard for inquiry and where assessment practices are well-established. As such, responses to criticisms require an in-depth examination of how design thinking approaches are implemented. While each context is unique, the change resistance of academia suggests that a design thinking approach is likely to be more useful in higher education contexts. Simply put, there are opportunities unique to higher education that include

- an ability to draw on best practices from empirical research to bring more validity to the design thinking approach; and
- intentionally criticizing the effectiveness and outcome of the design thinking process itself and documenting this criticism.

In addition, the following considerations should be made to improve the possibility of successful outcomes:

- Consider who is selected to lead and participate on a design team for any given innovation project and how they embody power and privilege.
- Pay close attention to consultations with and inclusion of members of the population to ensure that the design team is appropriately representative before the team is assembled and the process begins.
- Acknowledge bias in the process and take intentional steps to bring awareness to the individual and group biases that exist on the team and throughout the process.
- Expand the empathy building research to include perspectives of the population impacted by the end design, but also learn about context and consult stakeholders who have a role in the final decisions and/or implementation of the design to ensure feasibility and viability.

In a 2017 *Censemaking* article entitled "Beyond Bullshit for Design Thinking," Curtis Norman suggested ways that design thinking can go beyond hype and bring value. Drawing inspiration from best practices in research, Norman presented the following opportunities for teams of design thinkers to deepen their practice:

Show the work: Peer-reviewed empirical publications allow academics to see how a researcher concluded and to assess how reasonable that claim is based on the evidence presented. Design thinkers are increasingly tackling more complex problems, and in doing so must learn to better document the problem-solving process and use evidence to support decision-making. This documentation becomes the back up support for the implementation of the idea and records how critical feedback from various stakeholders was incorporated throughout each iteration of the process. By showing their work, design thinkers can gain credibility through transparency.

Articulate the skill set and toolset: Norman pointed to the importance of ensuring that the team assembled for a design project is not only diverse in their identity representation, but also their skill set. It is important to have an interdisciplinary team with a high level of skills relevant to the project. For example, if a team is working on a health-care-related project, it is important to have design team members with expert knowledge of this area. Norman also emphasized the importance of facilitation skills in design thinking to any type of project. Given the importance of team ideation and prototyping sessions, having an expert facilitator on the team is essential for success.

Develop theory: Norman noted that there is an opportunity for design thinkers to develop a theoretical base for cause-and-effect relationships that arise through the process. He emphasizes that theories can act as guides to bring focus to the most important information and goes on to suggest that an increase in the focus on scholarship and evidence-based research around design thinking will build a base of evidence to support possibilities for the most effective implementation.

Create and use evidence: In a similar vein, there is a gap in the research about the use and impact of design thinking. Challenges in carrying out this research, Norman suggested, are the complexity of the design process, a resistance to studying it by some designers because of overinflated claims of what it can accomplish, the designers' lack of training and experience in research methods, and the cost of undertaking this kind of research. Despite these challenges, creating evidence in support of design thinking and its most effective applications is a clear opportunity.

Evaluate impact: To understand the impact that design thinking is making in the world, it must be evaluated. Evaluation, Norman suggested, gives tools to help understand the impact of the innovation. Traditional models of design thinking have not incorporated evaluation and assessment. The lack of evaluation of evaluation and assessment in design thinking is why the authors of this book propose that the design thinking assessment model is so powerful.

Add value: Norman emphasized the importance of adding value, or rather that the result of a design process is something that creates value and change for the end users.

Norman's critical approach to the design thinking process provided many helpful points in response to some of the most prominent design thinking criticism. By reflecting on best practices from academic research, designers can refine and deepen their practice through an increased understanding of when design thinking works, why it works when it does, and evaluating the impact of the outcomes produced by the process.

There has also been criticism around design thinking's tendency to be conservative and protect the powerful. In these cases, critics argue, design thinking ultimately risks preserving the status quo. The authors would argue that this criticism may be true in some cases and that the antidote rests in the competency of the designers within principles of equity, the methods and quality of data collection during the empathy phase of the design process, and the focus on building an inclusive process that generates empathy for end users. There are important considerations that designers must make to ensure that they do not inadvertently preserve the status quo.

First, it is important for consideration to be given to who will lead a design team. As has been suggested in earlier chapters, it is ideal if design team leadership can consist of people who are members of the population for which the team is designing. In cases where this is not possible, it is important to ensure that consideration is made for how the leadership can establish an authentic relationship with the population, as well as all possible ways to include them in the process in a meaningful way. The goal is to empower the end users so that they can provide critical input and feedback throughout all phases of the project. Ideally, design teams should be led by someone who is willing to take a critical and objective look at the status quo and empowered to challenge it.

While it is impossible to completely avoid bias in the process, design teams should be built with the acknowledgment that certain members may have more power than others in an organization, and there is a high likelihood that those power dynamics will play out in the design process as well. While bias cannot be eliminated, recognizing and acknowledging biases through an explicit process will reduce their unseen impact and allow for intentional mitigation. Differential power dynamics and systems of power and oppression should be named as well for similar reasons. Consciously taking steps to consider these important criticisms while building the design team can mitigate some of the risk of protecting the powerful and perpetuating the status quo. Concerns about power and privilege are not unique to design thinking, and leaders would be well-advised to consider these steps in any spaces where decisions are being made on behalf of a population.

Critics have argued that design thinking is too vague and overinflates claims that it can solve all problems. Design thinking is simply one approach to problem-solving and certainly has its limitations. Rather than a one-size-fits-all approach, design thinking is just one method in a tool kit of approaches for problem-solving, and more importantly, empathizing with users.

Criticism that design thinking places too much emphasis on the person being designed for and does not pay enough attention to context and change management is worthy of consideration. One way to mitigate this challenge is to ensure that assessing the feasibility and viability of solutions is not an afterthought to desirability, but rather, that all three are considered in the empathy phase. Research for a design project is not required to be limited to hearing from the people that the solution will be designed for, but also others who have a stake in the final design. For example, those who will be responsible for implementing the solution, financing the solution, and others who have a stake in the solution should also inform the empathy phase of the project. Early feedback from these stakeholders can inform ideation as much as the initial data collected in the insights phase does.

Regarding Jen's argument that design thinking lacks criticism, this chapter illustrates that there has been some thoughtful critique of design thinking in informal publications and articles. Ongoing critique with reflection is important. In the spirit of iteration and IDEO's (2019) fail fast philosophy in design thinking, there is a case to be made for the constant criticism and reevaluation of design thinking as a model. Constant criticism and failure are built into most design thinking models with an emphasis on exploration through the prototyping and testing phases. By doing so, designers are encouraged to see failure as learning that leads to designs that are more desirable, feasible, and viable for implementation. So, while the design process itself may lack critical academic research to support it, frequent failure and making changes as learning and exploration happens is deeply embedded in the model.

During all the design thinking criticism, design firm IDEO spoke to *Fast Company* magazine in 2018 to share thoughts in response. IDEO reinforced that some of the design thinking criticism is valid as many have taken elements of the process and use it with a shallow approach, such as putting markers and Post-it notes in the boardroom to spark brainstorming and calling it design thinking, without focusing on the empathy generation phase. IDEO asserted that design cannot become too rigid, but rather needs to be fluid and flexible to become infused into an organization's culture (Schwab, 2018). Design is more about creativity than a rigid process, but the method does offer some structure for this process. IDEO argued against making design formulaic but rather suggests that the process offers milestones for creativity that can prevent design thinking from becoming reactive and soulless (Schwab, 2018).

IDEO mentioned factors for success including trust among coworkers to engage in such a creative process, having a culture that somehow authentically promotes play and joy as these are conditions for creativity to happen, and a willingness to embrace ideas and actually bring them to life rather than just trying to automate innovation. They continued that just because some designers or companies are doing design poorly, it does not invalidate the method itself and argues that the method cannot be judged on whether there is a successful product or service implementation at the end of each process because there are a number of factors that contribute to these outcomes (Schwab, 2018).

In his 2019 opinion piece entitled "Exploring the Reasons for Design Thinking Criticism," Shane Ketterman identified four strengths of the design thinking process:

1. Inclusive design—the design thinking process unleashes creative energy through brainstorming sessions and group involvement. The inclusive design approach is often described as a democratic process where the gap between designers and users is closed, helping to destroy top-down thinking and create diversified solutions.
2. Problem synthesis—design thinking employs a user-driven set of criteria that is approached with a blend of logical, linear thinking. To find the real problem, designers use these criteria to discover causality.
3. Diverse voices—the ideation phase of design thinking invites people from various backgrounds and includes them in brainstorming sessions which enhances the creative process by supporting a divergent set of ideas.
4. Low-risk—design thinking is a low-risk process. The only thing invested is a set of ideas. Nothing has been built and no money has been spent developing solutions that require an outlay of cash and resources. (para. 3) Design thinking takes time, which is also a valuable resource.

A fundamental advantage or feature of design thinking is its philosophy of inclusive codesign, designing with the end users rather than for them. Ketterman (2019) also shared some of the benefits of design thinking, citing the fact that bringing the end user into the process as a codesigner is a feature of design thinking. Ketterman emphasized that inclusive design generates energy in group sessions and welcomes divergent perspectives and is a key benefit of design thinking, along with its ability to distill problems using data. Risks in adopting a design thinking approach are relatively low and nothing is lost in exploring a new set of ideas through the process.

In the same article, Ketterman (2019) presented a Strengths, Weaknesses, Opportunities, and Threats (SWOT) analysis of design thinking. Strengths included the ability of design thinking to bring a creative lens to problem-solving that helps to dissect business problems so that they can be better understood. The low-risk nature of design thinking was also cited as a strength as well as its inclusivity and emphasis on generating ideas from a variety of different voices. Weaknesses identified were the linear or structured depiction of the process that in practice is quite nonlinear. These representations risk reducing the process to limited thinking. The unfortunate practice of using design thinking as a check box for corporations and the lack of criticism in industry for doing so were also cited as weaknesses. Ketterman mentioned a number of opportunities that design thinking has, including its ability to bring diverse people together for idea generation and as a process that includes structured practical steps for solving complex problems along with an understanding of stakeholder needs. Finally, Ketterman noted several threats to design thinking including its popularity (having become a buzzword), which opens it up to criticism and attack. The threat that design thinking loses relevance when seen as a corporate check box and the lack of solid theory and/or understanding of what design thinking is were also mentioned.

Ketterman (2019) emphasized that design is about creating conditions for investigations of problems where divergent voices are welcome and encouraged. He concluded that design thinking has fallen victim to popularity but that a human-centered approach to solving problems is not meant to replace traditional design processes that allow diverse voices to converge in problem-solving efforts.

As with many approaches to innovation, design thinking is not without its criticisms and challenges. Despite the criticisms, design thinking remains an inclusive, robust approach to problem-solving. The remainder of this chapter briefly outlines some challenges of implementing a design thinking process and offers opportunities to mitigate them.

Challenges with Design Thinking

Design thinking is a creative approach to innovation even with the criticism of it. There are also several challenges to consider when implementing a design thinking approach. The following pages offer a brief overview of some of the most common challenges with design thinking and thoughts for responding to those challenges. Generally, challenges can be categorized into three areas: resource challenges, capacity challenges, and cultural challenges.

Resource Challenges

The primary consideration for the implementation of any project is resources, with time, financial, and human resources being important factors in decisions around if and when to embark on a design think-ing project. When done well, design thinking takes time and space to allow for deep inquiry into current experiences of a given population, as well as investigation of context around the issue being explored. Teams must be assembled with diversity in skills and expertise and given time to deeply explore the topic at hand and the factors surrounding the issue. Additionally, teams will require time for creative thought, with an empha-sis on the necessity of failure in the process. While design thinking does not usually require expensive material to carry out, financial considerations must be made in terms of the investment in human resources to carry out the process and loss of productivity costs in cases where employees are transplanted from other roles and their day-to-day functions must be carried out by someone else.

Given that design thinking places an important focus on empathy build-ing, some attention should be given to decisions around whether to compen-sate participants for their time in interviews and testing of prototypes and other design-related activities. As with other assessment initiatives, providing some compensation to participants for their time and energy, particularly where participants are students, supports equitable best practices.

Depending on the organizational context, budget, and complexity of the problem needing a solution, resources may or may not pose a challenge. However, many student affairs units operate with tight budgets, and under-taking a design thinking process may prove resource intensive.

Capacity Challenge

Design thinking requires dedicated time and resources, and capacity constraints often go together with resource considerations. Today's postsec-ondary students are facing increasingly complex challenges while attending college or university, and many student affairs units struggle to meet demand for existing services given existing resources. Student affairs offices also encounter competing priorities as there are often multiple priorities compet-ing for attention and resources. Amid this, it may seem counterintuitive to decide to prioritize a design thinking process that demands capacity.

Alternately, design thinking helps student affairs units learn to do different things differently, argue Smith et al. (2015), consultants from New Campus Dynamics, an organization that supports institutions of higher education to build an innovation culture. Smith et al. suggested that the world and students are changing rapidly with opportunities for transforma-tion in higher education, and these changes and opportunities for transfor-mation call for innovation. Thus, the case for design thinking during capacity challenges creates an opportunity to rethink things and innovate.

Cultural Challenge

Many of the critics of design thinking have suggested that a process cannot change an organizational culture and that organizations must be readied for change. Any institution considering a design thinking process should examine the cultural readiness for exploration and change. The best ideas in the world may be generated through the process, but design thinking requires change management and a degree of culture change, which does not occur overnight.

Moving Forward with Design Thinking

Despite criticism and challenges, the authors believe that design thinking and the design thinking assessment process offer sound methods for innovation and collaboration appropriate for many of the wicked problems affecting colleges and universities. With appropriate leadership, design team capacity, and resources, the process could forge innovations in higher education.

Leadership and Championing

Implementing a design process effectively requires adequate championing and leadership. Support in terms of public commitment, dedicating time to go through a design process, as well as the financial and human resources required to go through the process is essential. The design thinking process works best when the team consists of members with interdisciplinary and complementary skill sets as well as expertise in areas that influence the question or problem at hand and that these team members have the capacity of time and resources required to focus on this work for a predetermined period of time. A transformational leader who consistently reminds the stakeholders involved with, or who has influence over, the proposed design can make a positive difference on the project's likelihood to succeed.

Building Design Team Capacity

The success of design thinking assessment implementation rests on both group and individual capabilities of the design team. The institution leadership must give thought to who the team members will be and what resources they will be given. In some cases, students, staff, and faculty can come together to form design teams. The more diverse the members, their identities, their perspectives, and their talents, the better. An effective design thinking process requires a well-resourced team who have opportunities for practice and skill building over time. Considerations need to be made for hiring faculty and staff dedicated to this work or reallocation of other job responsibilities to ensure ample time for focusing on the design thinking assessment work. Special attention must be paid to the design team membership and leadership and their relation to the student population for whom they are designing. Ideally, every effort should be made to ensure that there is representation from students who self-identify as members of the population who are end users, and that thought is given to strategies for feedback from end users.

Success of the design thinking process depends on building the capabilities of the team. For institutions that have no internal design thinking expertise, they should consider what training opportunities exist for the method itself and who should receive training. Beyond training, practice provides the most essential opportunity for skills development. Opportunities should be provided for team members to practice and hone their skills over time starting with lower stakes projects and moving to higher stakes.

Design thinking is not a once and done solution and one cannot become a design thinking expert by taking a short bootcamp-style training session. Institutions who commit to design thinking need to understand that the design team must be equipped with opportunities to hone their design skills. Carissa Carter, the director of teaching and learning at Stanford's d.school, wrote an article addressing this topic in 2016 where she compared the advancement of one's design skills to cooking. Carter explained that designers start out like a cook following a recipe. The design thinking method helps them to understand the usual flow of the process. However, over time, and through practice, the goal is to shift away from process toward ability where, in her cooking analogy, practice in carrying out the design thinking steps creates a transformation that can be likened to the shift from cooking with a recipe to cooking like a chef. The d.school emphasized eight abilities that designers shall acquire to increase creative confidence and approach difficult design challenges (Carter, 2016):

1. Navigating ambiguity—the ability to work in situations where all details are not known and develop one's own ability to move forward by reframing problems and finding patterns in data.
2. Learning from other people and contexts—the ability to empathize with other people and contexts and developing increased sensitivity to the experiences of others.
3. Synthesizing information—the ability to take complex qualitative and quantitative information and make sense of it to find opportunities to move forward.

4. Rapid experimentation—the ability to move from theory to action quickly by doing rather than thinking, making concepts tangible in a way that allows testing and feedback.
5. Moving between abstract and concrete—the ability to diverge and converge one's thinking to see both the details and the bigger picture, and to see the connectivity between all things.
6. Craft and create with intention—the ability to bring ideas to life to show the work to potential user groups in a way that it can be most quickly and easily interacted with to create feedback opportunities.
7. Deliberate communication—the ability to communicate findings and other information in a variety of ways and adapt communication to suit the needs of a particular audience.
8. Designing design work—the ability to bring tools and intuition together to make decisions about which tools, people, techniques, and processes will be best suited to address a particular design challenge. (para. 3)

The goal of competency development in design thinking is to move design team members from a focus on following the steps of a process toward the development of a set of creative skills that they will intuitively bring into their day-to-day work.

Resources for Design Thinking

Resources for the design thinking process must be considered as has been mentioned. Where possible, a budget for the design team should be issued and clear guidelines established for its implementation. In some cases, resources may be very constrained. In design, this is a creative challenge that poses an opportunity. The authors, however, would argue that a strong design team with time dedicated to this process proves an essential resource to the success of the project. Expecting team members to balance participating in this process amid full-time job obligations hinders success. As such, the authors recommend that team members have ample time dedicated to carrying out this process and that this is well-defined as part of the process budget.

Conclusion

Despite many criticisms and limitations, the authors believe that higher education practitioners are well-served to add design thinking to their tool kit. Design thinking offers many practical strategies for defining and ultimately working to solve complex and wicked problems that other methodologies lack. When implementing a design process, institutional leaders and design thinking teams will be wise to be mindful of some of the limitations and criticisms of design thinking and develop a plan to mitigate these in their process implementation. One of the greatest benefits of design thinking is that inclusivity and diversity are essential to the process. Design thinking proves most effective when members of the team self-identify as members of the community who will ultimately benefit from the end product or design. Divergent voices are a benefit rather than a limitation in the process. Design thinking is a powerful tool for solution development and change.

8

PULLING THE PIECES
TOGETHER

Alignment of Design Thinking and Student Affairs

D esign thinking is an innovative approach to problem-solving that has multiple applications to student affairs. The most obvious is the development of programs and services to address student needs and foster student learning and development. Design thinking can be implemented inclusively to ensure a myriad of voices are heard in the process of understanding what the true problem is that needs to be solved. Thus, students are part of the problem identification process and this is not solely left to administrators and their implicit biases. Students are involved in the ideation phase similarly to how research participants are involved in action research solving an issue in their community. Students are also involved as prototype testers providing useful feedback to continually tune the solution developed.

Cultural change is needed for design thinking, but design thinking can also foster organizational change. Design thinking fosters a systems approach to organizational effectiveness because it highlights the interconnection of various components of a problem and the many facets of the solution(s). One cannot implement design thinking without understanding how systems work. Colleges and universities are complex systems. Cohen et al. (1972) called colleges and universities organized anarchies. This is still an accurate description of higher education, with colleges and universities being kingdoms composed of various fiefdoms which are loosely federated and allegiant to a distant king, but also operate independently. Design thinking can unite seemingly disparate departments toward a common goal. Through empathy, design thinking can define common language, beliefs, symbols.

Diversity, equity, and inclusion are paramount values in student affairs as practitioners strive to provide opportunities for all students regardless of their identities. Design thinking supports these goals by ensuring voices of all users (students) are included to solve a problem. The approach reinforces the importance of involving diverse perspectives not just because it is inclusive, but because soliciting these perspectives leads to better solutions.

Finally, design thinking can be applied to assessment practices. When assessment is considered as a continuous cycle that includes outcome identification, strategies for outcome achievement, data collection and analysis, and use of data to effect change, it becomes easy to see how design thinking is a natural overlay onto traditional assessment processes in higher education. The steps of design thinking assessment include:

- empathy
- defining goals and outcomes
- brainstorming and ideation
- prototyping
- assessment
- storytelling

The design thinking assessment cycle is not necessarily linear as there may be internal loops with brainstorming influencing goals and outcomes, assessment influencing brainstorming and prototyping, and so on. Design thinking assessment is a more inclusive and equitable approach than what is typically implemented in higher education. Prototyping is a step in design thinking assessment that is absent in other forms of assessment. Prototyping is a more efficient use of resources and encourages risk-taking as well as failure. Design thinking assessment also has a focus on telling a story rather than simply reporting data. Stories include voices and people whereas data often denotes statistics. Applying design thinking to traditional assessment can revolutionize how programs and services are evaluated.

Integration of Design Thinking Into Student Affairs

To integrate design thinking into student affairs work there are a few steps that can be considered, including: providing professional development, making time for the approach, supporting culture change, and researching the impact of the approach.

Professional development is needed to help practitioners develop the skills and knowledge to use design thinking. Training can take many forms including individual reading and research, webinars, online workshops and courses, sessions at regional and national professional conferences, and stand-alone institutes. These professional development opportunities could be offered by institutions as credit-bearing courses or certificates. Professional organizations may also wish to offer these types of activities as free benefits for their members in addition to being revenue streams.

Design thinking fosters culture change, but also requires culture change to be sustainable. A culture audit or inventory that makes explicit the assumptions, beliefs, values, language, norms, and so forth operating within the organization can be a valuable tool to support culture change for design thinking. Those cultural elements must be named if they are to be adapted for design thinking. It is important to remember that culture change may take 3 to 5 years or longer. Thus, development of a multiphase culture change plan may be helpful. A culture change plan could begin with a focus helping practitioners develop empathy skills. Another step in facilitating culture change is increasing cultural competence of staff so that they can be more inclusive and make equity a hallmark value of the organization. Organizational leadership can reward risk-taking and failure as another phase in the plan since these are important steps for innovative program and service development. To effect equitable practice, current methods must be disrupted. Prototyping should also be encouraged as it can be a more efficient approach to resources as MVPs are implemented with a sample before fully scaling a program or service. Through the prototyping process, the program or service can be refined based on feedback from a sample and those revisions can be incorporated before a full rollout to all students.

A criticism of design thinking is that it is a time-consuming process. But many high quality and inclusive processes are time-consuming. Design thinking will more likely be implemented if there is a way to address the time challenge. A change to design thinking requires a mind shift. Student affairs professionals are continually being asked to do more with less. Being effective with limited resources necessitates intentionality and the ability to work smarter, not harder. Professionals in student affairs often use the buck-shot approach, trying a lot of different strategies hoping one of them reaches the target. The buckshot approach is an inefficient use of time and money. Staff need to stop programs, services, and practices that are not effective or not achieving stated outcomes (which requires assessment). Thought must be put into implementing strategies that have a high return on investment of resources regarding program and learning outcomes. The use of literature and research to guide practice is one way to do this. Finally, design thinking is just one tool in the toolbox for program development. It should be used for complex issues and to ensure an equitable solution. Other program development processes can be used for other issues.

Lessons Learned

Design thinking is a practice that requires ongoing learning and challenges the practitioner to step outside of their comfort zone and really connect with humans and their experiences. Each of the authors has had some degree of experience with design thinking and in the following pages we offer first-person insights into the most significant lessons we have learned in our journeys.

Julia

The years that I have practiced design thinking and trained students in this method and mindset have been filled with more learning than I can possibly transpose on to these pages. I can summarize the key lessons learned in a few key points. First, I have learned that failure is really hard for people, especially in our higher education context. I have also learned that the best outcome of design thinking is people and culture change, not great innovative stuff. Finally, good leadership is essential to the design thinking process. In the following pages I offer a few of my personal insights into these lessons. I write this with a caveat that each day I continue to learn so much in this work, and what if I had written this a year ago, or if I were to write this a year from now, these lessons would likely be different, but as of today, I offer these thoughts.

Failure is really hard for people, especially in the higher education context. Students come to the academy to pursue knowledge and learning. Faculty members are expected to be experts in their field, to know more about their field of research or practice than anyone else, and to continue advancing that knowledge through research and publication. Grades are the currency of institutions of higher education. When we look at the context in which we study and work, we can see many reasons why failure is not just hard, it is often perceived as forbidden. This poses a challenge when it comes to working with our community in the fail-forward, fail-fast, fail-often mindset required to do design thinking well. Every time I reflect on this, I think it is ironic that failure is so challenging because the purpose of any scientific experiment is also to fail and learn and try again. Yet somehow running a new pilot program for students and not having the uptake or seeing that a major change to a service needs to happen if you're the person who designed it—these are really hard for people in our context.

The best outcomes of design thinking are the changes to people, and ultimately to institutional culture, not just the innovations that are developed. Every innovative product, service, resource, space, or other end product of the design process will have an expiration date. However, the changes that happen when people engage in design processes and when the results of the empathy building work they do with humans are shared within a community—to me, this is what design thinking is truly about. In my work at the University of Toronto Innovation Hub, this is something I have seen play out over and over.

No student comes into this work and leaves unchanged in some way, or without some new understanding about people and their needs, and why empathy matters. No senior administrator who sees a presentation that offers personas, or human stories based on the data, and journey maps of someone's real journey through a problem or situation isn't moved by this information. Design thinking offers something different. It gets beyond your mind and into your heart. It connects people to our common struggles and common joys and reminds us that no matter what our roles are in life and in work, at the core, we all experience the same deep needs.

When the Innovation Hub was started, we hosted a large event where well over 250 students, faculty, staff, and others from the University of Toronto community were invited to take part in a day-long launch event. During this event there were presentations about design thinking and remarks from senior leaders introducing this concept of design thinking and why it is so needed in our community. During that event, tables of people were asked to brainstorm on a question: *What do students need in order to live a good life?* This question started a journey of crowdsourcing data that eventually led to the creation of the Innovation Hub's five domains: Access for Every Student, Fostering Connectedness, Future-Ready Students, Integrated Learning Experience, and Whole Student Development. These domains were written in an aspirational way to describe a future state that we collectively hoped to achieve at our institution if our design thinking processes were successful. They also gave scope to our work and our first design thinking teams were formed around these topics.

Starting in the fall of 2016, our first five design thinking teams, composed of both students and staff, got to work and carried out a design thinking process. At the time my design thinking knowledge was still developing and I was fortunate enough to work with Rotman I-Think to support training and coach our teams. By early 2017 the teams had completed their design thinking processes and each had five big ideas to improve campus life at the university. We held another large event to share back these ideas and solicit community participation in bringing some of the ideas to life. During the presentations when team members read quotations from students that illustrated the insights they generated by the data, you could feel a shift in the room. This was something different. I remember a senior leader telling me after that event that one of the things that dawned on them was that to hear survey data is always insightful, but to hear the stories moves your heart and you get a new understanding. This was an important moment for me because I realized that design thinking and the knowledge it generates through human stories moves people. This heart-tug moment that happens—and I have seen this over and over again—that ah-ha moment, it compels people toward action. After having this moment, they can no longer just continue to do what they are doing. Something has to change. Slowly, when enough people have these moments, the culture starts to shift and change.

Strong leadership is essential to the design thinking process. Design thinking is real work for the teams involved, and the work is emotional at times because we are working with people and with their stories. When I think about leadership for design thinking I think about this in two ways. The first is high-level leadership or championing that supports the resources required to carry out the design thinking process. The second type of leadership is the day-to-day leadership that is required to support design teams and hold the space for the work. What I have learned is that leadership in this context needs to look mostly like servant leadership. As a leader of design thinking teams, my role is to help people see their potential and use their strengths, both at an individual level and at a team level. I believe that this kind of leadership helps people see who they really are during the process and helps people stick with it when things become difficult. One could argue that this level of leadership is helpful in all team settings, and this may be true. My final thought on lessons learned is that creating safer spaces and encouraging people through the phases of this process and helping them to gain the confidence to bring their full selves into the work is an important role that cannot be neglected.

Lesley

I have learned a great deal about design thinking from my coauthor Julia, who taught me that design thinking is about changing people as much as it is about developing solutions. As I have grown to understand the process, it has deeply shifted the ethos from which I approach my work. For the past 5 years I have worked with teams of creative writers, designers, multimedia specialists, and social media managers serving student affairs and I have had the pleasure of seeing design processes in motion as we build materials and digital solutions to share the story of our colleagues' work. What I have learned is that communication is fundamentally about relationships, and any product created from a creative process is only as strong as the relationship between the designers, the colleagues we work with, and the audiences that our deliverables are for.

I have also had the privilege of connections with Indigenous colleagues and teachers who have helped me understand the importance of relationship and reciprocity in how we build and measure. We have already said this many times in the book, but here it is again. Design thinking on its own will not build long-term relationships, fix equity, or decolonize our institutions. We must each take continual steps toward building more competency in equity and in understanding our colonial systems. As we do that, we will interact with design thinking differently, and paired together, we can become powerful change agents that build solutions disruptive to harmful norms.

Through this process of learning, I have more deeply understood that extra time taken to do something right is worthwhile, even in our time-pressed, resource-stretched student affairs work. I have been part of cobbling together so many programs to align with a new strategy, or to be eligible for a new grant, and sometimes these things bring more problems than they solve. Design thinking has provided a very important structure that requires us to include extra time into our creative process to ensure we are truly centering students. Sometimes in our busy, reactive work we can forget that being student-centered means having students at the table. I am excited to see how we can use this process to embrace a nonhierarchical ethic of creation in partnership with the students we serve.

Gavin

I continue to learn from Julia and Lesley, not only about design thinking, but the underlying concepts and values. The focus on empathy and inclusion further my exploration of equity in assessment. Julia and Lesley's continual centering of Indigenous knowledge systems drove me to learn more about this. Lesley's model of design thinking assessment allowed me to see beyond traditional assessment cycles to what else is possible when practitioners and scholars integrate knowledge from other disciplines. Design thinking has had a cascading effect, furthering my knowledge in a number of areas.

Conclusion

Today's challenges in higher education call for different approaches to solving wicked problems. The preceding pages demonstrate that new mindsets are required to solve these problems. Design thinking is an emerging topic in student affairs. As such, it is important to evaluate its effectiveness. Evaluation requires assessment of the process itself. The question of return on investment must be addressed. In other words, is the result of using a design thinking approach worth the time and resources required? In addition, the fidelity of the process needs to be studied to ensure that it is implemented effectively and efficiently and to provide guidance on how to do so. There may be ways to productively implement design thinking but decrease the number of resources needed.

There will always be complex problems in higher education, but it may not always be feasible to implement a full-scale design thinking process. Even when a full design thinking process cannot be employed, having a design thinking mindset can help frame problems and solutions differently. In addition, parts of the design thinking process as well as specific strategies can be utilized. An entire decision thinking process does not always need to be used.

Design thinking can transform student affairs work and ensure inclusive and equitable experiences for students. The process will take some effort by practitioners, but students will benefit.

REFERENCES

ACPA-College Student Educators International. (2019). A bold vision forward: A framework for the strategic imperative for racial justice and decolonization. Author. https://www.myacpa.org/sites/default/files/SIRJD_GuidingDoc2.pdf

Acton Institute. (2020). *Lord Acton quote archive.* https://www.acton.org/research/lord-acton-quote-archive

Alderman, D., Perez, R. N., Eaves, L., Klein, P., & Muñoz, S. (2019, September 1). Reflections on operationalizing an anti-racism pedagogy: Teaching as regional storytelling. *Journal of Geography in Higher Education, 45*(2), 186–200. https://doi.org/10.1080/03098265.2019.1661367

Almeida, F., Faria, D., & Queirós, A. (2017, September 7). Strengths and limitations of qualitative and quantitative research methods. *European Journal of Education Studies 3*, 369–387. https://doi.org/10.5281/zenodo.887089

American College Health Association. (2016). *Spring 2016 reference group data report.* https://www.acha.org/documents/ncha/NCHA-II%20SPRING%202016%20US%20REFERENCE%20GROUP%20DATA%20REPORT.pdf

American College Health Association. (2020). *Spring 2020 reference group data report.* https://www.acha.org/documents/ncha/NCHA-III_SPRING_2020_REFER-ENCE_GROUP_DATA_REPORT.pdf

American College Personnel Association & National Association of Student Personnel Administrators. (2015). *ACPA/NASPA professional competency areas for student affairs practitioners* (2nd ed.). Authors. https://www.naspa.org/images/uploads/main/ACPA_NASPA_Professional_Competencies_FINAL.pdf

Andreas, S. (2018). Effects of the decline in social capital on college graduates' soft skills. *Journal of Industry and Higher Education, 32*(1), 47–56. https://doi.org/10.1177/0950422217749277

Antoine, A., Mason, R., Mason, R., Palahicky, S., & Rodriguez de France, C. (2018). *Pulling together: A guide for curriculum developers.* https://opentextbc.ca/indigenizationcurriculumdevelopers/

Arminio, J. L., & Hultgren, F. H. (2002). Breaking out from the shadow: The question of criteria in qualitative research. *Journal of College Student Development, 43*(4), 446–460. https://doi.org/10.1177%2F0950422217749277

Arum, R., & Roksa, J. (2011, January 18). Are undergraduates actually learning anything. *Chronicle of Higher Education.* https://www.chronicle.com/article/are-undergraduates-actually-learning-anything/

Battarbee, K., Fulton Suri, J., & Gibbs Howard, S. (2015, January 1). *Empathy on the edge: Scaling and sustaining a human-centered approach in the evolving practice of design.* https://new-ideo-com.s3.amazonaws.com/assets/files/pdfs/news/Empathy_on_the_Edge.pdf

Bear, L. L. (2000). Jagged worldviews colliding. In M. Battiste (Ed.), *Reclaiming Indigenous voice and vision* (pp. 77–85). UBC Press.

Behal, C. (2019, April 1). *Design thinking: A key to improving organizational culture.* Design and Innovation. https://www.designinnovationglobal.com/events-design-thinking/blog/design-thinking-a-key-to-improving-organizational-culture#:~:text=Design%20thinking%20is%2C%20in%20fact,its%20core%20philosophy%20and%20culture

Ben-Haim, Y. (2018). Positivism and its limitations for strategic intelligence: A non-constructivist info-gap critique. *Intelligence and National Security, 33*(6), 904–917. https://doi.org/10.1080/02684527.2018.1471846

Bernal, D. D. (2002). Critical race theory, Latino critical theory, and critical raced-gendered epistemologies: Recognizing students of color as holders and creators of knowledge. *Qualitative Inquiry, 8*(1), 105–126. https://doi.org/10.1177/107780040200800107

BFI Institute. (n.d.). *About Fuller.* https://www.bfi.org/about-fuller

Bingham, C. (2020, February 25). Affirming identity + cultivating humility for co-creative, inclusive learning. *Medium.* https://medium.com/equal-space/affirming-identity-cultivating-humility-for-co-creative-inclusive-learning-8b7025e6bfa

Board of Innovation. (2019, July 31). *Our favorite ideation tools.* https://www.boardofinnovation.com/staff_picks/our-favorite-ideation-tools/

Bresciani Ludvik, M. (Ed.). (2016). *The neuroscience of learning and development: Enhancing creativity, compassion, critical thinking, and peace in higher education.* Stylus.

Bridges, W. (2009). *Managing transitions: Making the most of change.* Da Capo Press.

Brinkhurst, M., Rose, P., Maurice, G., and Ackerman, J. D. (2011). Achieving campus sustainability: Top down, bottom up, or neither? *International Journal of Sustainability in Higher Education, 12*(4), 338–354. https://doi.org/10.1108/14676371111168269

Brown, S. (2019, September 11). *In the news: What's the value of design thinking?* https://www.devbridge.com/articles/value-of-design-thinking/

Brown, T. (2009a). *Change by design.* HarperCollins.

Brown, T. (2009b, July). *Designers—think big.* [Video]. TED Conferences. https://www.ted.com/talks/tim_brown_designers_think_big?language=en

Buchanan, R. (1992). Wicked problems in design thinking. *Design Issues, 8*(2), 5–21. https://doi.org/10.2307/1511637

Carroll. A. (June 9, 2020). *Understanding identity, power, & equity in design leadership* [Video]. Vimeo. https://vimeo.com/427590444

Carter, C. (2016, October 11). Let's stop talking about THE design process. *Medium.* https://medium.com/stanford-d-school/lets-stop-talking-about-the-design-process-7446e52c13e8

Cary, V., Malarkey, T., Anaissie, T., Clifford, D., & Wise, S. (2016). *Liberatory design card deck.* https://www.nationalequityproject.org/tools/liberatory-design-card-deck

Chessman, H., & Taylor, M. (2019, August 12). College student mental health and well-being: A survey of presidents. *Higher Education Today*. https://www.high-eredtoday.org/2019/08/12/college-student-mental-health-well-survey-college-presidents/

Cohen, M., March, J., & Olsen, J. (1972). A garbage can model of organization choice. *Administrative Science Quarterly, 17*(1), 1–25. https://doi.org/10.2307/2392088

Cooper, M. A. (2010). Investing in education and equity: Our nation's best future. *Diversity and Democracy, 13*(3). https://www.aacu.org/publications-research/periodicals/investing-education-and-equity-our-nations-best-future-0

Crabtree, M. (2017, May 31). 8 ways to fail your way to success. *IDEO*. www.ideo.com/blog/8-ways-to-fail-your-way-to-success

Creative Reaction Lab. (2018). *Equity-centered community design field guide*. https://www.creativereactionlab.com/our-approach

Creative Reaction Lab. (2019, October 16). Young Leaders for Civic Change: Eliminating gun violence use design to address gun violence. *Medium*. https://medium.com/equal-space/young-leaders-for-civic-change-eliminating-gun-violence-use-design-to-address-gun-violence-d4674aa3eb6a

Cross, N. (1982). Designerly ways of knowing. *Design studies, 3*(4), 221–227.

Cross, N. (2011). *Design thinking: Understanding how designers think and work*. Berg.

Culp, M., & Dungy, G. (2013). *Building a culture of evidence in student affairs: A guide for leaders and practitioners*. NASPA-Student Affairs Administrators in Higher Education.

Dam, R., & Siang, T. (2019a). *Stage 3 in the design thinking process: Ideate*. Interaction Design Foundation. https://www.interaction-design.org/literature/article/stage-3-in-the-design-thinking-process-ideate

Dam, R., & Siang, T. (2019b, November 22). *Stage 2 in the design thinking process: Define the problem and interpret the results*. Interaction Design Foundation. https://www.interaction-design.org/literature/article/stage-2-in-the-design-thinking-process-define-the-problem-and-interpret-the-results

Dam, R., & Siang, T. (2020a, June). *Proto typing: Learn eight common methods and best practices*. Interaction Design Foundation. https://www.interaction-design.org/literature/article/prototyping-learn-eight-common-methods-and-best-practices

Dam, R., & Siang, T. (2020b, August). *What is ideation—and how to prepare for ideation sessions*. Interaction Design Foundation. https://www.interaction-design.org/literature/article/what-is-ideation-and-how-to-prepare-for-ideation-sessions

Dam, R., & Teo, Y. S. (2020). *Design thinking: Get a quick overview of the history*. Interaction Design Foundation. https://www.interaction-design.org/literature/article/design-thinking-get-a-quick-overview-of-the-history

De Munck, V. C., & Sobo, E. J. (Eds.). (1998). *Using methods in the field: A practical introduction and casebook*. Rowman Altamira.

Denison, D., & Mishra, A. (1995). Toward a theory of organizational culture and effectiveness. *Organization Science, 6*(2), 147–239. https://doi.org/10.1287/orsc.6.2.204

Deschamps, T. (2015, March 16). Ryerson University vice-provost heads back to school to connect with students. *Toronto Star.* https://www.thestar.com/

yourtoronto/education/2015/03/16/ryerson-university-vice-provost-heads-back-to-school-to-connect-with-students.html?rf

Design Thinkers Academy. (2018, June 4). *Resist jumping to ideation & prototyping.* https://www.designthinkersacademy.co.uk/accidental-design-thinker/

Donati, C., & Vignoli, M. (2015). How tangible is your prototype? Designing the user and expert interaction. *International Journal on Interactive Design and Manufacturing (IJIDeM), 9*(2), 107–114.

Douglas-Gabriel, D. (2020, September 24). College enrollment takes a hit this fall amid coronavirus. *The Washington Post.* https://www.washingtonpost.com/education/2020/09/24/college-enrollment-coronavirus/

D'Souza, L., Smeed, J., Henning, G., Doerr, D., Hannah, J., Ellis, T., Willis, D., Parnell, B., & Wickiam, V. (2018, June 17–20). *What design thinking approaches to assessment can do for equity—design thinking assessment* [Conference session]. Canadian Association of College & University Student Services (CACUSS) Annual Conference, Charlottetown, PWI, Canada.

Dykes, B. (2016, March 31). Data storytelling: The essential data science skill everyone needs. *Forbes.* https://www.forbes.com/sites/brentdykes/2016/03/31/data-storytelling-the-essential-data-science-skill-everyone-needs/#6c59c8e352ad

Eines, T. F., & Vatne, S. (2018). Nurses and nurse assistants' experiences with using a design thinking approach to innovation in a nursing home. *Journal of Nursing Management, 26*(4), 425–431. https://doi.org/10.1111/jonm.12559

Emerson, R. M., Fretz, R. I., & Shaw, L. L. (2001). Participant observation and field notes. In P. Atkinson, A. Coffey, S. Delamont, J. Lofland, & L. Lofland (Eds.), *Handbook of Ethnography* (pp. 352–368). SAGE. https://dx.doi.org/10.4135/9781848608337.n24

Espinosa, L. L., Turk, J. M., Taylor, M., & Chessman, H. M. (2019). *Race and ethnicity in higher education: A status report.* https://1xfsu31b52d33idlp13twtos-wpengine.netdna-ssl.com/wp-content/uploads/2019/02/Race-and-Ethnicity-in-Higher-Education.pdf

Evans, N. J., Forney, D. S., Guido, F. M., Patton, L. D., & Renn, K. A. (2009). *Student development in college: Theory, research, and practice.* Wiley.

Ewell, P. (2007). *Applying learning outcomes concepts to higher education: An overview. A report prepared for the University of Hong Kong Grants Committee.* National Center for Higher Education Management Systems (NCHEMS). https://inside.southernct.edu/sites/default/files/a/inside-southern/assessment-and-planning/Applying-Learning-Outcomes-Concepts-to-Higher-Education-An-Overview.pdf

Fernandez, D., Fitzgerald, C., Hambler, P., Mason-Innes, T. (2016). *CACUSS student affairs and services competency model.* https://www.cacuss.ca/Student_Affairs_and_Services_Competency_Model.html

Fernandez, K., Wise, S., & Clifford, D. (n.d.). *Empathy techniques for pursuing educational equity.* K12 Lab Network, Stanford d.school, Carnegie Foundation.

Frey, C. (2020, April 2). The 7 all-time greatest ideation techniques. *Innovation Management.* https://innovationmanagement.se/2013/05/30/the-7-all-time-greatest-ideation-techniques/

Fuller, R. B., & Southern Illinois University World Resources Inventory. (1967). *Comprehensive design strategy.* https://www.bfi.org/sites/default/files/attachments/literature_source/wdsd_phase2_doc5_intro_ds.pdf

Godin, S. (2019, July 7). *'Scrappy' is not the same as 'crappy.'* https://seths.blog/2019/07/scrappy-is-not-the-same-as-crappy/

Goffee, R., & Jones, G. (1998). *The character of a corporation.* Harper Business Press.

Haber, J. (2020, March 2). It's time to get serious about teaching critical thinking. *Inside Higher Ed.* https://www.insidehighered.com/views/2020/03/02/teaching-students-think-critically-opinion

Hanington, B., & Martin, B. (2012). *Universal methods of design: 100 ways to research complex problems, develop innovative ideas, and design effective solutions.* Rockport Publishers.

Harrington, C. (2019, September 24). Towards equitable design when we design with marginalized communities. *Medium.* https://medium.com/acm-cscw/towards-equitable-design-when-we-design-with-marginalized-communities-c2f447f21568

Head, E. (2009). The ethics and implications of paying participants in qualitative research. *International Journal of Social Research Methodology, 12*(4), 335–344. https://doi.org/10.1080/13645570802246724

Henning, G., & Roberts, D. (2016*). Student affairs assessment: Theory and practice.* Stylus.

Henry, F., Dua, E., Kobayashi, A., James, C., Li, P., Ramos, H., & Smith, M. S. (2017). Race, racialization, and Indigeneity in Canadian universities. *Race Ethnicity and Education, 20*(3), 300–314. https://doi.org/10.1080/13613324.2016.1260226

Hester, K. S., Robledo, I. C., Barrett, J. D., Peterson, D. R., Hougen, D. P., Day, E. A., & Mumford, M. D. (2012). Causal analysis to enhance creative problem-solving: Performance and effects on mental models. *Creativity Research Journal, 24*(2–3), 115–133. https://doi.org/10.1080/10400419.2012.677249

Hiatt, J. M. (2006). *ADKAR: A model for change in business, government, and our community.* Prosci Learning Centre.

Hiatt, J. M., & Creasey, T. J. (2003). *Change management: The people side of change.* Prosci Learning Center.

Hogeveen, J., Inzlicht, M., & Obhi, S. S. (2014). Power changes how the brain responds to others. *Journal of Experimental Psychology: General, 143*(2), 755–762. https://doi.org/10.1037/a0033477

Holcomb, S. (2020, April 30). *Design thinking bootleg.* Standford d.school. https://dschool.stanford.edu/resources/design-thinking-bootleg

Holliday, B. (2018, December 1). *Ambiguity and design.* Leading Service Design. https://medium.com/leading-service-design/ambiguity-and-design-35e1982e855e

Horn, M. (2018, December 13). Will half of all colleges really close in the next decade? *Forbes.* https://www.forbes.com/sites/michaelhorn/2018/12/13/will-half-of-all-colleges-really-close-in-the-next-decade/#50870f8052e5

Huppatz, D. J. (2015). Revisiting Herbert Simon's "Science of Design." *Design Issues, 31*(2), 29–40. https://www.mitpressjournals.org/doi/pdf/10.1162/DESI_a_00320

Hussain, S. T., Lei, S., Akram, T., Haider, M. J., Hussain, S. H., & Ali, M. (2018). Kurt Lewin's change model: A critical review of the role of leadership and employee involvement in organizational change. *Journal of Innovation and Knowledge, 3*(3), 123–127. https://doi.org/10.1016/j.jik.2016.07.002

IDEO. (2015). *The field guide to human centered design.* https://www.designkit.org/resources/1

IDEO. (2016, January 1). *The little book of design research ethics.* https://lbodre.ideo.com/.

IDEO. (2019, April 4). *What is design thinking?* https://www.ideou.com/blogs/inspiration/what-is-design-thinking

IDEO. (2020a). *IDEO design thinking.* https://designthinking.ideo.com

IDEO. (2020b). *History.* https://designthinking.ideo.com/history

IDEO Inc. (1994, January 1). *Ideo Inc.* https://web.archive.org/web/20100817055141/http://findarticles.com/p/articles/mi_gx5202/is_1994/ai_n19122362/

IDEO U. (2017, September 27). *How to create change in your organization.* https://www.ideou.com/blogs/inspiration/how-to-create-change-in-your-organization

IDEO U. (2020). *Brainstorming—rules & techniques.* https://www.ideou.com/pages/brainstorming-rules-and-techniques

Iskander, N. (2018, September 5). Design thinking is fundamentally conservative and preserves the status quo. *Harvard Business Review.* https://hbr.org/2018/09/design-thinking-is-fundamentally-conservative-and-preserves-the-status-quo

Jacoby, A. (2017, September). Reframing the problem: Design thinking essentials. In C. Loue & S. B. Slimane (Eds.), *European Conference on Innovation and Entrepreneurship* (pp. 314–322). Academic Conferences International Limited.

Jen, N. (2018). *Design thinking is B.S.* [Video]. YouTube. https://www.youtube.com/watch?v=_raleGrTdUg

Kahneman, D. (2011). *Thinking, fast and slow.* Macmillan.

Kelley, T. (2018, November 7). Build your creative confidence: Empathy maps. *IDEO Blog.* https://www.ideo.com/blog/build-your-creative-confidence-empathy-maps

Kelley, T., & Kelley, D. (2013). *Creative confidence: Unleashing the creative potential within us all.* Currency.

Ketterman, S. (2019, March 28). Exploring the reasons for design thinking criticism. *Mobile design.* https://www.toptal.com/designers/product-design/design-thinking-criticism

Kezar, A. (2018). *How colleges change: Understanding, leading, and enacting change.* Taylor & Francis.

Knobloch-Westerwick, S., Mothes, C., & Polavin, N. (2020). Confirmation bias, ingroup bias, and negativity bias in selective exposure to political information. *Communication Research, 47*(1), 104–124. https://doi.org/10.1177/0093650217719596

Kolbert, E. (2017, February). Why facts don't change our minds. *The New Yorker.* taghttps://www.newyorker.com/magazine/2017/02/27/why-facts-dont-change-our-minds?mbid=social_twitter

Kotter, J. P. (1995). Leading change: Why transformation efforts fail. *Harvard Business Review, March–April,* 1–8.

Kwon, M., Lee, J., Lee, W., & Jung, H. (2020, April). BYE-TAL: Designing a smartphone app for sustainable self-healthcare through design thinking process. In *Proceedings of the 2020 Symposium on Emerging Research from Asia and on Asian Contexts and Cultures* (pp. 9–12). Association of Computing Machinery.

Laferriere, R., Engeler, B., & Rixon, A. (2019). Addressing cognitive challenges in applying design thinking for opportunity discovery: Reflections from a design thinking teaching team. *She Ji: The Journal of Design, Economics, and Innovation,* 5(4), 383–386. https://doi.org/10.1016/j.sheji.2019.11.012

Lauff, C. A., Kotys-Schwartz, D., & Rentschler, M. E. (2018). What is a prototype? What are the roles of prototypes in companies? *Journal of Mechanical Design, 140(6).* https://doi.org/10.1115/1.4039340

Lewrick, M., Link, P., & Leifer, L. (2020). *The design thinking toolbox: A guide to mastering the most popular and valuable innovation methods.* Wiley.

Libassi, C. (2018, May 23). The neglected college race gap: Racial disparities among college completers. *Center for American Progress.* https://www.americanprogress.org/issues/education-postsecondary/reports/2018/05/23/451186/neglected-college-race-gap-racial-disparities-among-college-completers/

Liedtka, J. (2018). Why design thinking works. *Harvard Business Review, 96*(5), 72–79. https://hbr.org/2018/09/why-design-thinking-works

Liedtka, J., & Ogilvie, T. (2011). *Designing for growth: A design thinking tool kit for managers.* Columbia University Press.

Ma, J., Pender, M., & Welch, M. (2016). Education pays 2019: The benefits of higher education for individuals and society. *Trends in Higher Education Series.* https://files.eric.ed.gov/fulltext/ED572548.pdf

Marcus, J. (2018, September 17). As students return to college, a basic question persists, what are they learning? *The Hechinger Report.* https://hechingerreport.org/as-students-return-to-college-a-basic-question-persists-what-are-they-learning/

Maslow, A. H. (1966). *The psychology of science: A reconnaissance.* HarperCollins.

McKinsey & Company. (n.d.). Enduring ideas: The 7-S framework. https://www.mckinsey.com/business-functions/strategy-and-corporate-finance/our-insights/enduring-ideas-the-7-s-framework

Mitchell, W. (2016). Developing multicultural competence for preparing student affairs professionals through a study away program. *Journal of College Student Development, 57*(8), 1056–1058. https://doi.org/10.1353/csd.2016.0100

Mojtahedi, A. (2019). 3 things design thinking can learn from action research. *Medium.* https://medium.com/design-bootcamp/3-things-design-thinking-can-learn-from-action-research-becc79d7472c

Mortensen, D. (2020a). *How to prepare for a user interview and ask the right questions.* Interaction Design Foundation. https://www.interaction-design.org/literature/article/how-to-prepare-for-a-user-interview-and-ask-the-right-questions

Mortensen, D. (2020b). *Stage 1 in the design thinking process: Empathise with your users.* Interaction Design Foundation. https://www.interaction-design.org/literature/article/stage-1-in-the-design-thinking-process-empathise-with-your-users

Moustakas, C. (1994). *Phenomenological research methods.* SAGE.

MSG. (2020). *Design thinking methods catalogue: Yes, and . . . msg.* https://www.designthinking-methods.com/en/3Ideenfindung/ja.html

Mulder, P. (2013). *ADKAR model by Jeff Hiatt.* https://www.toolshero.com/change-management/adkar-model/

NACE. (2018). *2018 job outlook survey.* Author.

National Center for Education Statistics. (2020). *Annual earnings by educational attainment.* https://nces.ed.gov/programs/coe/indicator_cba.asp

Norman, C. D. (2017, September 21). Design thinking is BS (and other harsh truths). *Censemaking.* https://censemaking.com/2017/09/19/design-thinking-is-bs-and-other-harsh-truths/

Office of Disease Prevention and Health Promotion. (2020). *Healthy people 2020.* https://www.healthypeople.gov/2020/leading-health-indicators/2020-lhi-topics/Mental-Health/determinants

Orensten, E., & Rubin, J. (2018, November 29). *Interview: Antionette Carroll, TED fellow and founder of Creative Reaction Lab.* https://coolhunting.com/design/antoinette-carroll-creative-reaction-lab/

Pearlstein, S. (2018, March 9). Is college worth it? One professor says no. *The Washington Post.* https://www.washingtonpost.com/business/why-higher-education-has-little-incentive-to-deliver-better-value/2018/03/08/a02684e0-224a-11e8-94da-ebf9d112159c_story.html

Perales, J. (2020, March 12). *Great questions lead to great design—A guide to the design thinking process.* Toptal. https://www.toptal.com/designers/product-design/design-thinking-great-questions

Peters, T. J., & Waterman, R. H. (1982). *In search of excellence: Lessons from America's best-run companies.* Harper & Row.

Pinedo, D. (2020, July 20). An introduction to liberatory design. *Medium.* https://uxdesign.cc/an-introduction-to-liberatory-design-9f5d3fe69ff9

Pink, S. (2016). Digital ethnography. In S. Kubitschko & A. Kaun (Eds.), *Innovative methods in media and communication research* (pp. 161–165). Palgrave Macmillan.

Polumbo, B. (2018, June 13). Why aren't college students learning anything? *National Review.* https://www.nationalreview.com/2018/06/learning-not-priority-for-college-students/

Pontefract, D. (2018, September 16). The foolishness of fail fast, fail often. *Forbes.* https://www.forbes.com/sites/danpontefract/2018/09/15/the-foolishness-of-fail-fast-fail-often/?sh=4839e3259d9b

Pope, R. L., Reynolds, A. L., & Mueller. J. A. (2019). *Multicultural competence in student affairs: Advancing social justice and inclusion.* Wiley.

Ries, E. (2011). *The lean startup: How today's entrepreneurs use continuous innovation to create radically successful businesses.* Crown.

Rith, C., & Dubberly, H. (2007). Why Horst W. J. Rittel matters. *Design Issues, 23*(1), 72–91. https://doi.org/10.1162/desi.2007.23.1.72

Rittel, H. W., & Webber, M. M. (1973). Dilemmas in a general theory of planning. *Policy Sciences, 4*(2), 155–169. https://doi.org/10.1007/BF01405730

Rowe, P. G. (1987). *Design thinking.* MIT Press.

RSA. (2013). *Brené Brown on empathy* [Video]. https://www.youtube.com/watch?v=1Evwgu369Jw&feature=youtu.be

Ryan, G. (2018). Introduction to positivism, interpretivism and critical theory. *Nurse Researcher (2014+), 25*(4), 14. https://doi.org/10.7748/nr.2018.e1466

Saldaña, J. (2015). *The coding manual for qualitative researchers.* SAGE.

Schein, E. H. (1996). Kurt Lewin's change theory in the field and in the classroom: Notes toward a model of managed learning. *Systems Practice, 9*(1), 27–47.

Schön, D. A. (1984). *The reflective practitioner: How professionals think in action.* Basic Books.

Schuh, J. H. (August 21, 2015). Assessment in student affairs: How did we get here? *Journal of Student Affairs Inquiry, 1*(1). https://jsai.scholasticahq.com

Schwab, K. (2018, October 29). IDEO breaks its silence on design thinking's critics. *Fast Company.* https://www.fastcompany.com/90257718/ideo-breaks-its-silence-on-design-thinkings-critics

Shapiro, E. (2019, March 1). Is the design thinking process bullshit? *Print.* https://www.printmag.com/design-criticism/design-thinking-process-bs/

Sheridan College. (2019, October 1). *Sheridan 2024: Galvanizing education for a complex world.* https://sheridan2024.sheridancollege.ca/img/Sheridan_Strat_Plan.pdf

Simon, H. A. (1969). *The sciences of the artificial.* MIT Press.

Sinek, S. (2009). *Start with why: How great leaders inspire everyone to take action.* Penguin.

Smith, L., & Blixt, A. (2015). *Creating an Innovation Hub: Chartering and staffing implementation teams.* New Campus Dynamics. https://www.academicimpressions.com/sites/default/files/InnovationHubArticle.pdf

Smith, L. N., Blixt, A. B., & Ellis, S. E. (2015). *Leading innovation and change: A guide for chief student affairs officers on shaping the future.* NASPA-Student Affairs Administrators in Higher Education.

Smith, S. M. (1997, October 4). The Satir Change Model. https://stevenmsmith.com/ar-satir-change-model/

Soule, K. E., & Freeman, M. (2019). So you want to do post-intentional phenomenological research? *The Qualitative Report, 24*(4), 857–872. https://search.proquest.com/openview/318344aba74157b83abac1a14db6652b/1?pq-origsite=gscholar&cbl=55152

Spector, J. (2016, October 25). How well you define a problem determines how well you solve it. *Medium.* https://medium.com/an-idea-for-you/how-well-you-define-a-problem-determines-how-well-you-solve-it-847090979898

Spurlock, R. S., & Johnston, A. J. (2012). Measuring a culture of evidence. In M. Culp & G. Dungy (Eds.), *Building a culture of evidence.* NASPA.

Stanley, N., & Dillingham, B. (2009). *Performance literacy through storytelling.* Maupin House.

Staton, B., Kramer, J., Gordon, P., & Valdez, L. (2016). *From the technical to the political: Democratizing design thinking* [Conference session]. Proceedings of Congreso International: Contested Cities, Madrid, Spain.

Stein, S. (2017, December 5). So you want to decolonize higher education? Necessary conversations for non-Indigenous people. *Medium.* https://medium.com/@educationotherwise/https-medium-com-educationotherwise-so-you-want-to-decolonize-higher-education-4a7370d64955

Stuckey, H. L. (2014). The first step in data analysis: Transcribing and managing qualitative research data. *Journal of Social Health and Diabetes, 2*(01), 006–008. https://doi.org/10.4103/2321-0656.120254

Szczepanska, J. (2019, June 2). Design thinking origin story plus some of the people who made it all happen. *Medium.* https://medium.com/@szczpan ks/design-thinking-where-it-came-from-and-the-type-of-people-who-made-it-all-happen-dc3a05411e53

Tagg, J. (2012). Why does the faculty resist change? *Change: The Magazine of Higher Learning, 44*(1), 6–15. https://doi.org/10.1080/00091383.2012.635987

Thaler, S., & Sunstein, K. (2008). *Nudge: Improving decisions about health, wealth, and happiness.* Yale University Press.

The Innovation Hub. (2019, April). *Making meaning at U of T.* http://blogs.studentlife.utoronto.ca/innovationhub/files/2019/08/MultiFaith_April2019-1.pdf

Transition Design Seminar. (2020, January 29). *Systems: Wicked problems, stakeholder relations.* https://transitiondesignseminarcmu.net/

Trelevean, S. (2018, December 7). How Canadian universities are responding to the TRC's calls to action. *Maclean's.* https://www.macleans.ca/education/how-canadian-universities-are-responding-to-the-trcs-calls-to-action/

Tull, A., & Medrano, C. I. (2008). Character values congruence and person-organization fit in student affairs: Compatibility between administrators and the institutions that employ them. *Journal of College & Character, 9*(3). https://doi.org/10.2202/1940-1639.1118

University of Toronto. (2020a, May 4). *Innovation Hub.* http://blogs.studentlife.utoronto.ca/innovationhub/

University of Toronto. (2020b, May 14). *Multi-Faith Centre for Spiritual Study & Practice.* http://blogs.studentlife.utoronto.ca/innovationhub/files/2019/08/MultiFaith_April2019-1.pdf

Vagle, M. D. (2018). *Crafting phenomenological research.* Routledge.

Van Tyne, S. (2016, November 20). *Viability, feasibility and desirability.* https://seanvantyne.com/2016/11/20/viability-feasibility-and-desirability/

Veblen, T. (1918). *Higher learning in America: A memorandum on the conduct of universities and business men.* B. W. Huebsch.

Vinsel, L. (2017, December 6). Design thinking is kind of like syphilis—It's contagious and rots your brains. *Medium.* https://medium.com/@sts_news/

design-thinking-is-kind-of-like-syphilis-its-contagious-and-rots-your-brains-842ed078af29

Vinsel, L. (2018, May 21). Design thinking is a boondoggle: Its adherents think it will save higher ed. They're delusional. *Chronicle of Higher Education.* https://www.chronicle.com/article/design-thinking-is-a-boondoggle/

Weiner, B. J. (2009). A theory of organizational readiness for change. *Implementation Science, 4*(67). https://doi.org/10.1186/1748-5908-4-67

Whearley, N. (2017, February 18). *History & approach.* https://dschool.stanford.edu/fellows-in-residence/project-fellowship-history-approach

Wilson, S. (2008). *Research is ceremony. Indigenous research methods.* Fernwood Publishing.

Wyman, N. (2018, August 3). Hiring is on the rise, but are college grads prepared for the world of work? *Forbes.* https://www.forbes.com/sites/nicholaswyman/2018/08/03/hiring-is-on-the-rise-but-are-college-grads-prepared-for-the-world-of-work/?sh=63f2bd134e7e

Zieman, G. A. (2012). Participant observation. In S. Klein (Ed.), *Action research methods: Plain and simple* (pp. 49–67). Palgrave Macmillan.

ABOUT THE AUTHORS

Julia Allworth is an equity-centered design thinker who strives to design *with* rather than *for* people. In 2016 Julia started the Innovation Hub at the University of Toronto, an on-campus consultancy where she leads interdisciplinary teams of students to find new solutions to wicked problems using design thinking. Julia also consults with senior leaders about how design thinking can be a human-centered method to create lasting organizational change. She holds a BA in psychology and an MBA and has presented her work at various higher education conferences across North America. Additionally, Julia has built an experiential curriculum for design thinking that has taught hundreds of students, faculty, and staff to carry out equity-centered design thinking processes.

Lesley D'Souza is a higher education leader specializing in student affairs and storytelling with data. Currently, she is the director of Strategic Storytelling & Digital Engagement in Western University's Student Experience division. After focusing on assessment and storytelling in her two previous roles, Lesley is exploring how data-informed stories can be used to intentionally shift culture in positive directions using digital engagement and communication best practices. Lesley has held leadership roles in the Canadian Association of College and University Student Services and ACPA–College Student Educators International. She engages in public speaking on topics such as equity and decolonization in assessment, women in leadership, and change management. She completed her MA in college student personnel from Bowling Green State University in 2006. She loves gardening, music, and mothering her two little boys.

Gavin Henning is professor of higher education and director of the EdD and MS Higher Education Administration programs at New England College in New Hampshire. Gavin has served as president of ACPA–College Student

Educators International and the Council for the Advancement of Standards in Higher Education. His publications include *Student Affairs Assessment: Theory to Practice* (2016, Stylus) coauthored with Darby Roberts. Gavin received a PhD in education and an policies studies and MA in sociology from the University of New Hampshire, and an MA in college and university administration and a BS in psychology and sociology from Michigan State University.

reflect mode, of the liberatory
design model, 66, 67–69
reframing process, problems within,
43–44
refreezing stage of change, 86
*Reimagine Learning and Education
in our Communities Challenge*
(Sheridan College), 96–97
research, secondary, 47–48
research question, within design
thinking, 21
resistance, roots of, 81
resource assessment, 114
resources, 29–30, 41, 114,
135–136, 139
retention, 1
return on investment, 148
Ries, Eric, 53
Rittel, Horst, 5, 15
Rowe, Peter, 16

Satir Change Management Model,
89–90
satisfaction assessment, 111
Schön, Donald, 16
scope assessment, 111
secondary research, 47–48
second-order change, 83, 92
self-awareness, 67
sensemaking, 84
Shapiro, Ellen, 128
shared values factor of change
management, 87
Sheridan College (Ontario,
Canada), 95–97
short-term wins, 88
Simon, Herbert, 15
Sinek, Simon, 30
situational awareness, 67
skills factor of change management,
87

social location, process of, 64
solutions, 5, 10, 61, 65
staff factor of change management,
87
stakeholders, 6, 11, 46, 54, 71, 130,
133
Stanford University, 17, 65–66, 78,
138–139
Start With Why (Sinek), 30
status quo, within design thinking,
127–128, 132
storytelling, 33, 46, 78, 93–94,
114–120, 142
Strange, Carney, ix
Strategic Imperative on Racial
Justice and Decolonization
(SIRJD), 59, 62–63
strategic planning, as assessment,
114
strategy factor of change
management, 86
structure factor of change
management, 86
student affairs: assessment
within, 99–102, 110–114;
challenges within, 136; culture
of evidence within, 80; design
thinking adoption within,
76–77, 100–101, 142–144;
design thinking within, 10–13,
102–104; diversity, equity, and
inclusion within, 142; empathy
exploration within, 106; equity
within, 59–60; needs assessment
within, 105; processes within,
2; prototypes within, 108–110;
representation within, 59;
values-based approach within,
62–63
student(s), xviii, 3, 5–6, 8–9,
19–20, 32, 141

Improving Student Learning at Scale

A How-To Guide for Higher Education

Keston H. Fulcher and Caroline O. Prendergast
Foreword by Stephen P. Hundley

Afterword by Natasha A. Jankowski

This book is a step-by-step guide for improving student learning in higher education. The authors argue that a fundamental obstacle to improvement is that higher educators, administrators, and assessment professionals do not know how to improve student learning at scale. By this they mean improvement efforts that span an entire program, affecting all affiliated students. The authors found that faculty and administrators particularly struggle to conceptualize and implement multisection, multicourse improvement efforts. It is unsurprising that ambitious, wide-reaching improvement efforts like these would pose difficulty in their organization and implementation. This is precisely the problem the authors address.

Infusing Critical Thinking Into Your Course

A Concrete, Practical Approach

Linda B. Nilson

"This book should be read and used by every faculty member. Improved critical thinking is an essential outcome for all courses and for research training in any field. Nilson has drawn on her long experience as an outstanding faculty developer to make it easier for any of us to foster advanced critical thinking. She clearly explains the underlying rationale and provides powerful ways to engage students. She includes: (a) a quick and accurate review of major alternative frameworks, (b) extensively developed examples of ways to implement each of them with students, and (c) multiple approaches to assess students' thinking while fostering further sophistication. I would have been a much more effective teacher if I had had this foundation to build on."
—*Craig E. Nelson, Professor Emeritus, Biology, Indiana University*

Facilitating the Integration of Learning

Five Research-Based Practices to Help College Students Connect Learning Across Disciplines and Lived Experiences

James P. Barber

Foreword by Kate McConnell

"*Facilitating the Integration of Learning* is one of the few books that delivers more than its title promises. The middle section of the book, chapters 4–8, does what the title describes: It offers five practices educators can implement to help college students integrate their learning. However, the book goes beyond that in two ways. First, Barber adds an informative and in-depth discussion of integrative learning in the first section of the book. Second, he examines ways to assure that integrative learning is a central feature of the student experience, considering both how to create an integrative curriculum and how to document and assess integrative learning as part of a broader effort of iterative improvement.

In summary, Barber's book provides a wonderful opening into a robust consideration of how individual faculty and other educators can facilitate students' integration of their learning. The book balances solid foundational considerations with practical tips and tools that are easy to implement."
—*Elon Center for Engaged Learning Book Review*

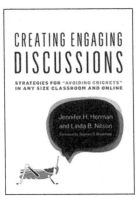

Creating Engaging Discussions

Strategies for "Avoiding Crickets" in Any Size Classrooms and Online

Jennifer H. Herman and Linda B. Nilson

Foreword by Stephen D. Brookfield

"*Creating Engaging Discussions* examines one of the most challenging parts of teaching—designing and managing discussion activities that engage students while contributing meaningfully to their learning. Faculty members will love the way the book addresses their common instructional challenges with a mix of evidence-based principles, use-it-on-Monday activities, and in-depth case studies. Educational developers will appreciate its scholarly background and suggestions for using the book within reading groups and workshops. A must-have addition for your bookshelf."—*Greg Siering, Director, Center for Innovative Teaching and Learning, Indiana University Bloomington*

Creating Wicked Students

Paul Hanstedt

"This book could be useful as an introduction to course design for someone less familiar with the fundamentals, such as how to develop measurable learning outcomes, align course goals with institutional goals, nest content within higher-order goals, engage students' prior knowledge, or incorporate applied learning. The structure of the book allows for one to follow it step-by-step as a course design manual, and it also includes recursive 'intermissions' to encourage reflection along the way. In addition, his discussion of how to prompt critical thinking through multiple-choice exams offers helpful strategies for encouraging students to explain their thinking on ambiguous questions with follow-up questions that explain or justify their choice."—*Reflective Teaching*

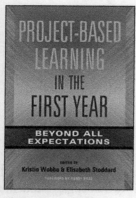

Project-Based Learning in the First Year

Beyond All Expectations

Edited by Kristin K. Wobbe and
Elisabeth A. Stoddard

Foreword by Randall Bass

Published in association with the
AAC&U

"This book offers a powerful rationale and supportive evidence for using project-based learning in the first year rather than in the traditional place as a capstone project, where students demonstrate their mastery of knowledge and skills developed earlier. Projects in the first year can offer a richer early college experience and the development of important professional skills like communication, persistence, and emotional intelligence. They also can lead to early opportunities for internships and more professional-level summer work, motivation for subsequent coursework, and the building of confidence and academic community through deep relationships with faculty and peers. I really like that each chapter ends with 'Try this!' prompts, which guides readers to the next steps needed for the adoption of particular tools and approaches in their own classroom, program, or university."—**Ken Bain**, *President, Best Teachers Institute*

COURSE-BASED
UNDERGRADUATE
RESEARCH
Educational Equity and
High-Impact Practice

Edited by NANCY H. HENSEL
Foreword by CATHY N. DAVIDSON

Course-Based Undergraduate Research

Educational Equity and High-Impact Practice

Edited by Nancy H. Hensel

Foreword by Cathy N. Davidson

Copublished With the Council on Undergraduate Research

"If you are an educator who believes in the importance of all students engaging in undergraduate research as a way to develop the competencies needed to thrive in an innovation-driven economy, then this book is a must-read. *Course-Based Undergraduate Research* provides practical, equitable, and inclusive strategies for making undergraduate research accessible and engaging for every student."—***Tia Brown McNair***, *Vice President, Office of Diversity, Equity, and Student Success, Association of American Colleges and Universities*

"This collection offers persuasive and ample evidence that undergraduate research opportunities can be embedded in all academic disciplines, in courses as diverse as biology, theater studies, history, and remedial study skills. The benefits are well-documented: richer learning outcomes, enhanced critical reading and thinking skills, deeper engagement, and increased collaboration." —***Michael J. McDonough***, *President, Raritan Valley Community College*

POGIL

An Introduction to Process Oriented Guided Inquiry Learning for Those Who Wish to Empower Learners

Edited by Shawn R. Simonson

"*POGIL* is a well-envisioned and superbly executed volume. Initial chapters lay a comprehensive theoretical and empirical foundation for the POGIL approach. The following chapters provide an accessible scaffolding for implementing POGIL. The book is full of usable principles and informative examples for developing POGIL across a variety of STEM and non-STEM courses, even for large classes. This volume is a gem both for readers wanting an introduction to POGIL and for readers poised to initiate and improve their POGIL instruction."—**Mark A. McDaniel**, *Codirector, Center for Integrative Research on Cognition, Learning, and Education (CIRCLE), Washington University in St. Louis*

Getting Started With Team-Based Learning

Jim Sibley and Pete Ostafichuk

Foreword by Larry K. Michaelsen

With Bill Roberson, Billie Franchini, and Karla Kubitz

"The book is full of practical advice, however, which is well-grounded in literature about teaching and learning so that faculty members who are hesitant to transform a course to TBL can still benefit from reading (advice such as how to write effective multiple-choice questions and how to facilitate discussions). After reviewing the book, I am motivated to try this model in my teaching."—**David B. Howell**, *Ferrum College, Wabash Center for Teaching & Learning in Theology and Religion*

(Continued from following page)

"With the overarching goal of assessment being directly tied to the improvement of student learning, this book reinforces the general idea of the more information a student has about him/herself, the way they learn, and the subject being studied, the more successful they will be in achieving academic success. The authors present a process (The Transparency Framework) that includes the who, what, when, where, and why of what a student is expected to learn and how a faculty member can help ensure they do. Their research shows that the model is adaptable to every class size and institutional type. While not the proverbial silver bullet, it comes as close in its practical implementation of research-based theories on student learning as I've ever seen."
—**Belle Wheelan**, *President and Chief Executive Officer, Southern Association of Colleges and Schools' Commission on Colleges*

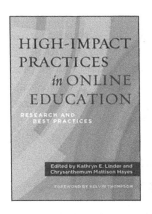

High-Impact Practices in Online Education

Edited by Kathryn E. Linder and Chrysanthemum Mattison Hayes

Foreword by Kelvin Thompson

"*High-Impact Practices in Online Education* allows faculty and staff to begin to think deeply about how these practices, which have largely existed in the traditional, face-to-face environment, can be adapted and applied to engage students across all learning modalities. With chapters dedicated to each high-impact practice, reference to existing research and best practice literature, and strategies to consider when scaling these practices to the online environment, this book will revolutionize high-impact practices as we know them by making them truly accessible to all students."—**Stephanie M. Foote**, *Assistant Vice President, Teaching, Learning, and Evidence-Based Practices, John N. Gardner Institute for Excellence in Undergraduate Education*

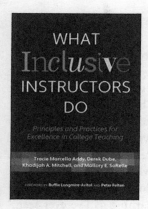

What Inclusive Instructors Do

Principles and Practices for Excellence in College Teaching

Tracie Marcella Addy, Derek Dube, Khadijah A. Mitchell, and Mallory SoRelle

Foreword by Buffie Longmire-Avital and Peter Felten

"This book is a timely and extraordinarily comprehensive resource for supporting instructors who wish to engage with inclusive teaching. Every facet of what makes teaching inclusive is unpacked and brought to life with quotes and examples from real instructors across different disciplines and institutional contexts, and the reflection questions embedded within each section create a natural way for instructors to engage more deeply with the text and think about applications in their own teaching. No stone is left unturned in connecting the practices shared and the research on why and how those practices support inclusion, making this a most valuable resource for instructors at any stage in their teaching careers."—*Catherine Ross, Executive Director, Center for Teaching and Learning, Columbia University*

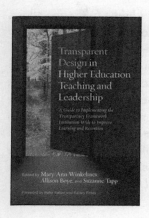

Transparent Design in Higher Education Teaching and Leadership

A Guide to Implementing the Transparency Framework Institution-Wide to Improve Learning and Retention

Edited by Mary-Ann Winkelmes, Allison Boye, and Suzanne Tapp

Foreword by Peter Felten and Ashley Finley

Continues on previous page

Overcoming Student Learning Bottlenecks

Decode the Critical Thinking of Your Discipline

Joan Middendorf and Leah Shopkow

Foreword by Dan Bernstein

"Middendorf and Shopkow provide an accessible and long-needed volume that speaks to both faculty and professional developers. Drawing on their expansive experiences and research, they articulate a wide range of contexts for applying the decoding methodology to strengthen faculty's epistemological underpinnings, transform teaching and learning, and inform strategies for curricular development. This valuable resource is accessible across disciplinary, institutional, and international contexts."—*Kathy Takayama*, *Director, Center for Advancing Teaching and Learning Through Research, Northeastern University*

Flipped Learning

A Guide for Higher Education Faculty

Robert Talbert

Foreword by Jon Bergmann

"Think you know what flipped learning is? Think again. I had to. It's not about technology, recording your lectures, or physical classrooms. This is why you have to read Robert Talbert's *Flipped Learning*. It's the definitive book on the pedagogy, with a new and refreshing perspective. Talbert relates flipped learning to theories of motivation, cognitive load, and self-regulated learning and gives step-by-step directions for flipping your course, along with plenty of examples, answers to typical questions, and variations for hybrid and online courses."—*Linda B. Nilson*, *Director Emeritus, Office of Teaching Effectiveness and Innovation, Clemson University*

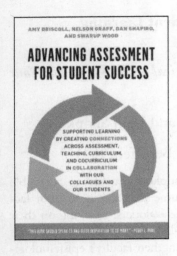

Advancing Assessment for Student Learning

Creating Connections / Cultivating Collaboration

Amy Driscoll, Nelson Graff, Dan Shapiro, and Swarup Wood

Foreword by Peggy L. Maki

This book is about student success and how to support and improve it. It takes as its point of departure that we—as faculty, assessment directors, student affairs professionals, and staff—need to reflect together in a purposeful and informed way about how our teaching, curricula, the cocurriculum, and assessment work in concert to support and improve student learning and success. It also requires that we do so in collaboration with our colleagues and our students for the rich insights that we gain from them.

Conversational in style, this book offers a wide variety of illustrations of how your peers are putting assessment into practice in ways that are meaningful to them and their institutions, and that lead to improved student learning. The authors provide rich guidance for activities ranging from everyday classroom teaching and assessment to using assessment to improve programs and entire institutions.

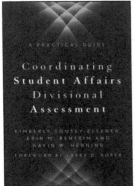

Coordinating Student Affairs Divisional Assessment

A Practical Guide

Edited by Kimberly Yousey-Elsener, Erin M. Bentrim and Gavin W. Henning

Foreword by Larry D. Roper

"[The] editors have provided a comprehensive guide for coordinating assessment within the complex organizational environments of student affairs divisions. Ostensibly written for newly hired assessment coordinators, the discussions of coordinators' responsibilities presented in this book will also be of interest to experienced incumbents as well as individuals aspiring to these unique roles. While intended for assessment coordinators, this volume is also essential reading for vice presidents and other senior student affairs leaders considering creating an assessment coordinator position or wishing to better understand the role. Faculty members teaching assessment courses may find that the applied nature of the book helps students connect key concepts to professional practice."
—*Teachers College Record*

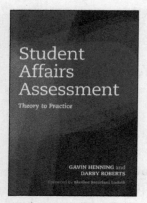